NOT QUITE AT SEA
BY GRAHAM DENT

ABOUT THIS BOOK

The author has never been to sea professionally, but has always been on the 'fringes' of the fleet, in his sport as a dinghy sailor, in his employment as an accounts clerk with the Port of London Authority and in his military service with the Royal Navy. Nevertheless, in all three of these activities he witnessed plenty of dramatic and humorous situations.

The book covers his adventures from early childhood to his thirties, with a final chapter that brings the reader more or less up to date.

THE AUTHOR

Graham Dent has been interested in nautical matters since the age of ten and is currently treasurer of the Society for Sailing Barge Research. He is also a Life Member of the Leigh-on-Sea Sailing Club and has served on its committee for long periods in the past. He worked for the Port of London Authority for 34 years and for Customs and Excise for seven years. He is married with two grown-up children and lives in Leigh-on-Sea, Essex.

The Essex marshes

Nick Hann collection

NOT QUITE AT SEA

GRAHAM DENT

ASHRIDGE PRESS

Published by
Ashridge Press
A subsidiary of Country Books

ISBN 1 901214 06 0

Design, typesetting and production:
Country Books, Little Longstone,
Derbyshire DE45 1NN

Printed and bound by: Antony Rowe Ltd, Chippenham, Wiltshire

IN MEMORY OF
MY MOTHER AND FATHER

FOREWORD

2003 is a sort of 'centenary 'for Leigh-on-Sea Sailing Club as its predecessor, the West End Sailing Club was formed in 1903. As part of the celebrations, I promised a book about the Club – not a full history for that will need much research and will appear for the 'official' centenary in 2011. A collection of yarns seemed appropriate and, when I started thinking about the project, it occurred to me that there was also plenty of material in the two years I spent as a National Serviceman in the Navy and my early days working for the Port of London Authority. So it is a bigger book, with photographs, supplied by many people who I thank for their kind assistance and acknowledge in the captions.

I hope that this expands the book's interest and does not detract too much from the original concept. And, I must mention many of the yarns are now quite old and have probably 'improved with the telling'.

G.E.D.

PROLOGUE

"What will you have?" my companion asked as we entered the bar of the 'Jolly Sailor' at Maldon.

"A pint of bitter, please."

"I would have thought that an old salt like you would have had rum."

Me, an old salt? I reflected later in my bunk on the sailing barge. I didn't qualify. I'd never been to sea professionally. Why, the furthest I'd been was a quick foray into the Atlantic on board an aircraft carrier. Most of my National Service had been onshore and most of my sailing only local, within a few miles of the shore. Even now, we were only taking the barge from Maldon to Gravesend, ready for the Thames Barge Match.

And yet I had probably seen and heard more drama and humour afloat and near the water than a professional might experience in a lifetime at sea. No grand events, no dramatic shipwrecks, but plenty of incident, both dangerous and humorous.

And then there were the characters I had met along the way – shortsighted Sid who helped teach me to sail, Roy Petrie and Leading Seaman Singer, two crafty helmsmen who had suffered me as crew, that bully of a Chief Gunnery Instructor who, never-theless had flashes of humanity. What was his name? Harry, the indestructible lighterage foreman, the martinet Dockmaster of West India Dock, his wife, Olive Oil, and many more.

Then there were the barges, like the one I was aboard now, trying to write my first novel. Perhaps there was a story in all this...

EARLY DAYS

It was my paternal grandfather who started my family's involvement with the water. There was a tradition of male members of the family managing a Greek bank in the City of London. But grandfather would have none of this and ran away to sea as cabin boy on a Cape Horner. Once his father got wind of the proposed adventure, he contacted the ship-owner and signed an indenture for grandfather to be an apprentice and possible future officer. He went round the Horn a couple of times and then came ashore to sit his Second Mate's ticket but at this point was lured into the family bank.

One of my father's earliest memories was of sailing with his father off the shore at Westcliff-on-Sea. This was a happy time for him as it was prior to his father's divorce, in those days a far more devastating event than it would be now. It was largely this memory that inspired him to move to nearby Leigh-on-Sea in the 1930s. There he bought Nimrod, a converted ship's boat in which he, my mother and friends had much fun until she was sold round about the time of my arrival.

'Nimrod'
Dent family collection

However my father did retain Nimrod's flattie dinghy, a vessel that was to have a very long life as she was still around on the Leigh foreshore after my father had sold his last boat in the 1970s. As the name implies she was completely flat bottomed and therefore not an easy vessel to row but she could hold four adults and was a useful tender to a larger boat. It was in this craft that my nautical career began.

During the Second World War the Southend district, which included Leigh, was considered a potential invasion area and most of the seafront was barricaded off and access denied to the public. This did not include the Leigh harbour area, which continued to be used by the fishing fleet and Thames barges, and the MTBs and MLs constructed by the local boat builder, Johnson and Jago. It also had to act as a 'beach' for the neighbourhood children, or at least those who had not been evacuated.

As the threat of invasion receded, my father refurbished Nimrod's dinghy. It was, of course, used only for rowing and most of our expeditions were upstream because of the closed seafront. These trips took us up the narrowing Leigh Creek that divided Two Tree Island

'Nimrod's' dinghy. My father rowing.
Dent family collection

from the mainland and eventually joined up with Benfleet Creek, which ran up to the village of that name. Two Tree Island takes its name from the two prominent trees that stood in the centre of the island. My father used to kid me that there had originally been three but that a cow had eaten one. Now, unfortunately there are none, unless you count a few stunted growths around the former sewage farm at the eastern end of the island.

In those days the row up Leigh Creek was idyllic with skylarks calling overhead and very little sign of human activity, if you discounted the odd courting couple and a few determined seawall walkers. Happily this is still true today, although cars can penetrate as far as the bridge that connects Two Tree to the mainland and gives access to the yacht moorings off the South Shore of the Island.

Just beyond the site of the present-day bridge was the wreck of a sailing barge, the Diligent of Faversham. In the 1940s her name and port of registry were clearly readable and she had her gear, mast, sprit etc, stowed on deck. In fact I'm not so sure that she didn't float on some spring tides! Local rumour says that she was originally moored off Leigh Old Town, but broke adrift in an easterly gale and ended up in this inland position. She is still there, but unrecognisable as a spritsail barge and is so overgrown that she resembles a marsh island. Close examination, however, will still reveal traces of the original woodwork.

Further up, just on the junction with Benfleet Creek, were the remains of a jetty, an ideal site for a picnic. This was the former Salvation Army Wharf, which serviced the Army's farms on Hadleigh Downs. It was no doubt used by sailing barges and similar vessels and was originally believed to have been connected to the farms by a light railway, which crossed the main London-Southend line by bridge.

Later on the restrictions on the use of the seafront were relaxed and my family was able to become a bit more venturesome in its rowing activities. On one notable occasion when the weather must have been very calm we went way beyond Two Tree Island and visited the eastern end of Canvey Island, known as Canvey Point. Here there was a beach, part sand and part cockleshells, but more importantly to a small boy the remains of an American bomber. I could remember seeing the parachutes float down when its crew baled out towards the end of the war. At least so I believed, but this may have been another aircraft on a different occasion. Anything of any value had already disappeared from the wreck, but there were still plenty of bits of loose, anonymous lumps of metal for a schoolboy to remove for the admiration of his schoolfellows. Years later, in the 1970s, I sailed over to the Point with my own family and still found traces of the bomber.

In 1947 my father decided to sell our house in Highlands Boulevard, Leigh and move to a fisherman's cottage in Old Leigh, the difference in the price of the two houses being used to finance the building of a new motor cruiser to his own design. The cottage, where my mother lived until recently, was on Church Hill that runs down from St. Clements Church towards the shore and was ideally suited to marine activities and close to Old Leigh's other attraction, several public houses! The cottage, one of a terrace of seven, was built around 1880 for the use of a fisherman's family and the centre bedroom contains a large cupboard over the stairwell, suitable for the stowage of nets or sails. Over the years the cottages have become residences for a variety of people, none of whom work on the water. They are now Grade 2 listed buildings, only St. Clements Church itself, the Crooked Billet Inn and the Old Bank House meriting Grade 1 in Old Leigh.

My father's new boat, to be named Islander, was built by Les Warland at his yard on Leigh Marshes. The yard consisted of a number of redundant Thames lighters, no doubt purchased at knockdown prices, which had had their swim bows cut off so that they could be used as small floating docks. The lighters were connected by planks at deck level to give access when the tide was high and the journey over several of them used to terrify me for I had no head for heights and I knew that a mistake on the planks could result in a plunge into either salt water or very soft mud. One lighter, with a shed aboard, served Les as an office and was a mass of paperwork, for although he was a very good boat builder, he was a poor businessman. When Les's finances were at low ebb he sometimes took on a partner, who would usually make things worse by appropriating either cash or supplies. Surprisingly, though, Les kept meticulous records in old exercise books of all the comings and goings at the yard and these would now make interesting reading if they had survived.

Progress on the building of Islander was erratic since the number employed at Warland's yard varied between none and a dozen according to the existing financial climate. To complicate matters still further, Les was also building a number of hard-chine, centreboard yachts around the same time. One of these, Boy Martin, was a gaff rigged, half-decked boat, but the others were Bermudan rigged and had small cabins. These yachts must have been well built for several of them were around many years later and Boy Martin is still sailing, until recently owned by the son of her original owner. Still eventually there was worth-while progress with Islander and I was taken to see her in a planked-up condition. But this was my last visit to the yard before she was complete, for what I thought were more pressing matters claimed me.

At this time, like many 11-year-old boys, I was an avid train spotter and much of my spare time was spent hanging around Leigh-on-Sea station taking engine numbers with several other lads on the same mission. The London, Tilbury and Southend Railway, part of London, Midland and Scottish was still steam hauled at that

Les Warland (with pipe) in conference
Dent family collection

'Boy Martin' when fairly new
Nick Hann collection

15

time and, apart from the regular service to Fenchurch Street, also carried trains from St. Pancras and Kentish Town together with weekend excursions to the holiday town of Southend from places like Tring in Hertfordshire. We train spotters were quite capable of spending most of the day waiting around in the hopes of spying an unusual engine pulling one of the excursion trains. Very often our only sustenance would be an ice-lolly bought from a floating café near the railway station. This vessel was a former Thames sailing barge but unfortunately I never noticed her name.

Train spotting was not without incident. We often had to abandon our perch on the road bridge alongside the station when a herd of cows from the nearby Theobald's farm was driven across the bridge to graze on the marshes. But at least we didn't suffer like the employees of Turnnidge, the local sail maker, who used to dress barge sails in a field that later became the site of the station. The field also contained Theobald's bull and the sail makers sometimes had to desert their sails and scramble on to the railway line for safety. From there they would throw flints at the bull to make it go away.

It was through train spotting that I missed Islander's launch. Some of us had decided to expand out horizons and visit Southend Victoria station, the terminus of the LNER route into the town. This had a nearby engine shed which was visible from the road and which promised to be a lucrative source of fresh engine numbers. Moreover some of the engines on this line actually had names! So far as I was concerned this expedition ranked as more important than the launching of a boat that was more my parents' concern. So although the launching, or rather floating since Les merely pulled the plug on the barge in which the boat had been built, was witnessed by uncles, aunts, cousins and, of course, my parents, I was missing.

Once fitted out, Islander became established on her mooring off my father's favourite watering hole, the Crooked Billet. She was an elegant-looking boat unless you viewed from the bows-on position, for she was rather beamy for her length. She was also of shallow draught, less than two feet. This was a distinct advantage in shoal water and she could even beat local fishing vessels up Leigh Creek on the first of the tide to gain the prime position off the Crooked Billet while waiting for enough water to gain the mooring. It could also be a disadvantage as she was apt to slam in any sort of sea and toss her propeller out of the water.

She was very comfortable below. There were bunks for four people – two in the foc'sle and two in the saloon, these doubling as settees during the day. An adequate galley with a stove and a water tank faced a toilet compartment amidships. A bookshelf contained pilotage volumes in addition to a book entitled 'The Life of Jesus' which my father intended to read one day but never got around to.

Her cockpit was spacious and could seat four people on a bench right aft over the fuel tank. Propulsion was by a Stuart- Turner eight horse-power engine that had an absolute luxury for those days – electric starting which only meant pushing a button. No swinging of starting handles! Sails were provided but owing to Islander's shallow draught and lack of any form of centreboard, could only be used in a following wind or as steadying sails in a blow.

Needless to say we started to go places in our new vessel. One immediate favourite was not far away. This was the Ray, proper name Hadleigh Ray, which leads to Benfleet Creek. It begins down towards Southend Pier and the tricky entrance to it, generally known as the low-way, is marked by the Leigh Buoy. At low tide the Ray becomes a long sheltered channel surrounded by banks of hard sand. The shelter provided by the banks is ideal for yachts to lie in at anchor and for dinghies to sail at times that they would not be able to use from the shore. The sandbanks are an ideal playground for children and have been used for numerous games of cricket, football and rounders. Swimmers, too, find the Ray useful for their sport and many walk out from the shore to take advantage of the deep water at low tide.

We also found an excellent weekend anchorage upstream under the lee of Canvey Point. This was sheltered from all wind directions except due east. There were deep pools where shallow draught vessels could remain afloat at low tide and the idea was to find one of these if possible, although a bar prevented access to the actual Ray from this position. The anchorage was quite rich in wild life – wading birds often visited and fish frequently jumped alongside. We got to know several 'regulars' in this haven, mainly boats that had dropped down from Benfleet for the night.

Later I found out that this area had seen quite a lot of commercial activity a few years earlier. Sailing barges used to pass this way on voyages to Benfleet or up the adjacent Smallgains Creek. Unwanted gasworks ashes were dumped on Bargander sand to the north by sailing barges, while yet more barges loaded sand from Leigh sand hill that was not far away. Now things have gone full circle with the anchorage busy again with the expansion of the Two-Tree moorings, which are full of yachts and commercial fishing vessels. The deep water holes are still much in demand as the site of these moorings.

Another regular trip was to Queenborough in Kent, a port that had a number of unusual features in those days. The most obvious was the glue factory that not only produced a distinctive odour but also made ominous noises during the night. There was also a large jetty occupying most of the seafront, which had been used as a minesweeper base during the war and was then disused. There was also a considerable commercial traffic of barges and quite large ships to Ridham Dock further up the River Swale. This combination of jetty and ship movements drastically reduced the space in which yachts could anchor for the night. Even then there was a further hazard in the shape of submarine cables on the bed of the harbour waiting to snag anchors.

On the plus side there was excellent landing on a hard that stretched almost to low water. Here small boys would guard your dinghy, moving it up or down the hard according to the tide. The hard gave access to the town where there were shops, including one that sold fish and chips and a quite disproportionate number of pubs, three of them being in the same block of buildings. Queenborough was sheltered from most winds, although a nasty popple could be knocked up when wind was against tide.

These days Queenborough is even more popular as a weekend anchorage. The jetty is gone and has been replaced by a large number of yacht moorings. The cables have also gone and the commercial traffic has decreased considerably. The original glue factory is no more but has been replaced by less smelly and noisy industry while the number of pubs has diminished, one becoming Queenborough Yacht Club and another a restaurant producing sustaining and inexpensive meals for yachtsmen.

It was at Queenborough that Islander nearly came to grief, through no fault of her own or her crew. It was breakfast time and the wind was

'Islander'

Dent family collection

already fresh enough for us to have doubts about sailing back to Leigh that day. Next to us a yacht was getting underway, its crew appeared only to be a man and a boy of about nine years old, probably his son. Since the hard part was raising the anchor the father went to do this, leaving the boy to steer and operate the engine. They evidently intended to sail once the anchor was stowed for the mainsail was already up.

The engine was put into forward gear to help break the anchor out. As the anchor broke clear the boat took on a sheer, the mainsail filled with wind and the yacht came straight into Islander with both engine and mainsail driving her. My father, who could not swim, was on deck and tried to fend the yacht off by pushing on her bowsprit but was dragged off by the rebound and ended up partially in the water, clinging to the bowsprit and in imminent danger of being crushed as the two boats swung together. Somehow, with help from the yacht, my mother and I managed to extricate him.

Although insurance details were exchanged, the owner of the other boat, once he realised that Islander was not in imminent danger of sinking, pleaded urgent business elsewhere and departed, leaving my mother and I to assess the damage. This was not great – a cracked window, a dented rubbing band and the loss of the ensign and its staff. But my father was a different matter. Once he had recovered from his partial immersion, it was evident that he had hurt his back, probably when the two boats swung together and was in need of a doctor. But how to get him to one? He was in too much pain to go ashore in the dinghy and it was unlikely that a doctor would come out to the boat and, of course, radio was unheard of on small craft in those days.

In the end it was decided that my mother would row ashore to summon Les Warland to help get Islander back to Leigh where my father would see his own doctor. Les, who was well used to helping his customers out of trouble, arrived a few hours later but decided that the weather was now too bad to cross the river. Instead he recommended that he pilot Islander into Queenborough Creek on the next high tide. The creek ran right up into the town and had berths alongside the quay. These were normally used by commercial craft but Les had noticed that several were vacant on his way through the town.

Once we berthed alongside, it was comparatively easy for a local doctor to visit. He pronounced father badly bruised and strained but raised no objection to the voyage back home once the weather moderated provided father rested and Les handled the boat. Some time later, Les detected a lull in the wind and we set out to cross the Thames. But if it was a lull, it was short – lived and we made a very rough crossing. So ended Islander's momentous weekend voyage.

There were several other ports that were visited less frequently. Hole Haven was on the south side of Canvey Island and, at that time, had a manned pier where the dinghy could be left in safety. One unusual pastime in Hole Haven Creek was watching unfortunates grappling for outboard motors that had become unshipped from dinghies.

Harty Ferry at the eastern entrance to the Swale had a pub that then could only be reached easily by water and therefore became a Mecca for yachtsmen and other water users. Now, unfortunately, a road has been opened up to it. Cockham Woods, near Upnor, home of the Medway Yacht Club, had a beach of sorts and woods that came down almost to the water's edge.

Annual holidays were also spent on Islander, several times on the upper Medway, visiting Maidstone and beyond in fresh water, since the river was non-tidal beyond the first lock at Allington. It was at Maidstone that I tried to rig the flattie dinghy for sailing. This eventually proved impossible since the little boat had no provision for a centreboard. Still I had a lot of fun with the project and it kept me amused for several hours.

Another year we ventured up the east coast as far as Pin Mill near Ipswich. We used the River Crouch as a starting point for this holiday, keeping Islander at Lion Creek, Wallasea Island, where Les Warland had some sort of sub-depot, for most of that season. This arrangement enabled us to explore the rivers Crouch and Roach prior to the actual holiday. In addition to Pin Mill we visited the Walton Backwaters where there was a good sandy beach at Walton Point and Brightlingsea where there was an argument as to whether Islander was subject to light dues or not. Finally we called at West Mersea just in time for the Town Regatta, which used a sailing barge, Ethel Maud from Maldon, as committee boat, probably one of the last occasions that this happened. Unfortunately bad weather prevented us from returning to the Crouch for a number of weeks, but the folk of West Mersea were very good, keeping an eye on Islander and ensuring that she was pumped out.

Round about this time a new hobby took over from train spotting. I was cycling home from school one day and as I came over the brow of Leigh Hill I looked down at the water and saw two sailing barges, Carina and Calluna, being assisted into Bell Wharf by two former sailing barges converted to full power, Queen and Pimlico. Now I had recently read a book about the Thames sailing barges and knew that there were not many of them left. To see two entering Leigh at the same time was unusual, moreover I knew from my reading that Carina and Calluna were units of the fleet of Goldsmiths of Grays, but here they were flying the flag of the London and Rochester Trading Company of Rochester. This, I decided, was worthy of investigation.

I soon found that Goldsmiths had sold what was left of their once considerable fleet to London and Rochester, which had a great deal of work on, delivering cement to the London Docks, although on the occasion I saw the four barges they were timber laden for delivery to Bell Wharf, Leigh's general cargo wharf. The other wharf, Theobald's, was operated by Leigh Building Supply for their own cargoes. I

Sailing barge 'Cambria' (Goldsmith)

Author's collection

vaguely remembered seeing sailing barges in large numbers at Theobald's but this must have been before Leigh Building Supply motorised their fleet, which still delivered timber and ballast under power.

So interested was I that I began making a note of all barge movements in and out of Leigh. Two more of the former Goldsmith barges, Cambria and Kismet, both with timber, soon rewarded me with visits. One of London and Rochester's wooden barges, Federation, came to Theobald's Wharf and left under sail going 'over the top', not leaving by Leigh Creek but sailing over the mud banks at high tide and thereby saving quite a bit of time. But most of the visitors were mere motor barges, either cut-down from sail or custom built. One of the former was James & Ann of Faversham, so recently reduced from sail that she still carried her leeboards. This must have been one of the last sightings of her for shortly afterwards she was run down and sunk with tragic loss of life on the Thames.

So keen did I become on this activity, that I soon extended it to cover the local fishing fleet and yachts and kept notebooks (some of which I still have) where everything was recorded. I also extended the barge part to cover nearby Southend. Here there was the Corporation Loading Jetty, which saw a few barges with timber and ballast and the Gasworks Jetty where craft of the River Lighterage Company discharged coal. Among the latter was Kentish Hoy, now fully powered, but which had started life as Goldsmith's Germanic. At the Loading Jetty Ashingdon, the last sailing barge to be owned in Southend, was a regular visitor and I was also fortunate to see Piper's M. Piper shortly before her career came to an end.

And, of course, the trips on Islander helped with the barge spotting. I was able to watch one of the early post-war Medway Barge Matches, then organised by the Marina Club, Hoo while we were anchored off Cockleshell Beach at Port Victoria on the Medway. The competitor that stood out was the elegant barge-yacht Thoma II with her clipper bow and white hull. She is now a motor yacht in the Mediterranean. Another Medway trip was rather sad I saw some of S. J. Brice's fleet, Nelson and GCB among them, discharging coal for Sheerness gasworks. As we went further up the Medway we met various motor barges coming the other way, but no sailing barges. At Rochester there was a sad sight – a number of the former Goldsmith barges lay on moorings, stripped of their sailing gear evidently only being used as dumb lighters. These included Senta, Yarana and Asphodel. Over at London and Rochester's yard another sailing barge, The Brownie, was being converted to power and, worst of all for me, the Southend Ashingdon also swung to a buoy, awaiting conversion to a yacht.

At Point Yard, just above Rochester Bridge and home of S. J. Brice's fleet, their Rowland and R.S.Jackson minus their sails, looked forlorn. Further up river I saw the former Goldsmith Astrild loading cement from the Cuxton cement works. Her sailing gear was down on deck, but it all seemed to be there and was probably only lowered to negotiate Rochester Bridge. She was the last sailing barge to be seen that trip and it was not long before most of the ex-Goldsmith barges went to the breaker's yard.

The years 1952 and 1953 were exciting ones at Leigh-on-Sea. First there was the great white-weeding craze. White-weed, or sea moss as it was sometimes known, was actually an animal not a vegetable. It lived on the bed of shallow estuaries like that of the Thames and its frond-like structure made it ideal as a decoration when dyed, usually green.

Fishermen have always caught some of it in their nets, but the first attempts to harvest it commercially were by divers actually going down to the seabed. But it was soon found that a better and more economic method was for it to be wrenched from the bottom by triangular shaped metal rakes, towed one each side of a vessel. The task of hauling in the heavy rakes could be made easier by adapting an old lorry axle to act as a winch.

Once these discoveries were made, the industry took off. Existing fishing boats, mainly shrimpers, were adapted for the new trade, although most took the precaution of retaining their original gear in case anything went wrong in their new livelihood. These boats were those of the traditional fishing families but the good money to be made from white weeding soon attracted non-professional fishermen in a great variety of boats. Motorised Yorkshire Cobles, Scottish Zulus and Fifties and Rye beach boats, to say nothing of the many converted lifeboats and adapted motor yachts, began working from Leigh and the fishing fleet more than doubled. Berths at Bell Wharf, where mooring was free for bona fide fishermen, were at a premium.

With so many boats and people involved it was not surprising that trouble eventually arose. There was a Klondike Gold Rush atmosphere about the whole business. Dealers in white weed would even roll up their trouser legs and wade into the creek as the tide made to plead with first boats home to sell them their catches.

It became accepted practice to add water to the catch before it was weighed to increase the poundage on which its value was calculated. Then there were the accusations of sabotage – sugar added to petrol tanks, unexplained fires aboard boats when nobody was about and so on.

Probably the most famous incident was involved the Radiant, which was more due to incompetence than wrongdoing. The Radiant was a large trawler of Scottish origins engaged in white weeding. She went aground on the edge of the Maplin sands and another white-weeding trawler went to her aid. A line was passed in an attempt to tow Radiant off but it was steel wire and when a coil of it tightened up round the legs of Radiant's mate it almost severed them. The trawler was abandoned and the crew taken aboard the other boat which radioed for medical assistance to meet her at the end of Southend Pier. On the way

On board white-weeding vessel 'New Pride of Essex'

Dent family collection

the injured mate asked the others to throw him overboard. They declined but in hospital the mate lost both legs. Later a dance was held at St. Clements Church Hall to help raise money for artificial legs for him and was a sell-out.

I did three trips after white weed, technically as a passenger, but I did give some help with 'culling' or sorting the catch. The first was on Sally Ann, a Southend beach boat with wheelhouse added for some protection. She was skippered by Les Warland in one of his many breaks from boat building. It was a rough trip and the only occasion when I have been seasick. I like to think that this was because Sally Ann had caught her trawl in a wreck and was rolling with a rather peculiar motion. Or it may have been something I ate! The second time was on a much bigger vessel, the New Pride of Essex, again a Southend beach boat but large enough to require three crew. Roy Edmondson, an engineer by trade, skippered her, and I believe my cousin and I received some small reward for our help. The third voyage was again with Les Warland, this time on a former Scottish trawler Rolling Wave and took

White weeding vessels at Bell Wharf, Leigh

Author's collection

place in idyllic conditions.

There was an American election going on at the time of the white weed boom and the weed was very popular in the States generally but eventually someone sent a batch of poorly dyed weed over there and that was the end of the good times. White weed hung on as a catch for many years but only as an alternative to other fishing. A few of the modern trawlers at Leigh occasionally trawl for it to this day.

On the 31st January 1953 the east coast was hit by a disastrous storm surge. Canvey Island was particularly badly affected with quite a few lives lost. Early the next morning I went for a walk through Old Leigh, not realising what had happened, but noting unusually large groups of fishermen hanging about. (I later learned they were waiting for transport to Canvey to assist in the evacuation.) I returned home and had sat down to breakfast when my father came downstairs and said that he didn't know how he was going to get to work the next day as the railway line was flooded up towards Benfleet. He had seen this from the bedroom window.

We had not finished breakfast when a Civil Defence worker knocked at the door. He knew my father personally and asked whether there was any chance that Islander could help in rescuing people from Canvey. Dad explained that his boat was laid up for the winter and would not float in her berth at Les Warland's until nearly high water. Moreover her engine had been dismantled and part of it had been sent to a garage for attention. The Civil Defence man then told us that Leigh's fishing fleet would be going over to Canvey on the tide to assist in rescue work and that crews would be needed. Could my father and I report to Bell Wharf with this in mind?

We did so, but the Sea Scout master who was in charge at the wharf, felt that I was too young to go to Canvey as "there were dead bodies floating about." Instead he asked me together with my cousin, who had also turned up, to remain at the wharf with our bicycles ready to run messages as required. I believe that we did run one each but they were nothing dramatic. My father went with Roy Edmondson on New Pride of Essex to Benfleet where they were needed to act as a ferry if the bridge to Canvey went underwater on the tide. But this didn't quite happen, so they had a fairly pleasant day drinking tea and playing cards and then returned.

When the immediate rescue work was over, great efforts were made to repair Canvey's broken seawalls before the next cycle of spring tides. To this end Bell Wharf was used for the filling of sandbags that were then shipped to the more inaccessible parts of Canvey by fishing boats. This, I believe, was quite lucrative both for the sandbag fillers and boat crews but, unfortunately, I was unable to join in since I was expected to attend the High School each day.

Later that year my cousin, Simon, acquired a small, gaff-rigged sailing dinghy called Siva and he and I had several exhilarating sails in her once we had, more or less, grasped the basics of sailing. We wanted to know more and this led to us joining Leigh Sailing Club.

JOINING LEIGH-ON-SEA
SAILING CLUB

My father had always maintained that one should never join clubs – "It only ends in trouble and rows." Indeed we already had an example of this with the strife that was caused by the politics of my uncle and aunt's tennis club. However, through his frequenting of the Crooked Billet, father came to know several members of Leigh-on-Sea Sailing Club and on one memorable Saturday morning was invited to transfer up to the club from the Billet to see what it was like. He came home after a very enjoyable time and admitted that he had completed the necessary application membership form while he was there.

My cousin Simon and uncle Herbert had already joined for sailing reasons and it was inevitable that I followed shortly, though I do remember Simon and I visiting the rival and older established Essex Yacht Club to see what that was like. Later my mother and aunt also joined, followed by Simon's brother, James, when he was old enough. This made the family quite a club 'clan'.

At the time we joined the club occupied roughly half the old railway station at the end of Old Leigh High Street, the other half being retained by British Railways as storerooms. The three rooms available (plus toilets) were the saloon, bar and a committee room-cum-office-cum-changing room. Heating was by a small electric fire in the bar (which was for the use of men only) and by a coal fire in the saloon. This was laboriously cleaned out and re-laid by the club's cleaner or, in her absence, by a club member. Heating in the committee room was non-existent, perhaps in the hope of speeding up meetings!

The club had started life as the West End Sailing Club to cater for the sailing needs of the 'professionals' – boat builders, sail makers, etc. The exact year is uncertain, being variously reported as the 1890s or 1903. This organisation became defunct about 1908, but was reformed with many of the same members in 1911 as Leigh-on-Sea Sailing Club (not to be confused with Leigh Sailing Club, a former name of the Essex Yacht Club and that of another club in Leigh, Lancashire). At

Leigh-on-Sea Sailing Club's headquarters in the old railway station

Author's collection

first the club met in premises on the Strand in Leigh Old Town but in 1922 acquired its first floating clubhouse, the Veronica, a vessel originally built as a convalescent home for soldiers returning from the Boer War. Although not very warm in winter this vessel proved a good clubhouse and it is rumoured that more beer was drunk aboard her without a licence than in the present clubhouse with one!

In 1937 Veronica was replaced by the former topsail schooner Lady Quirk that, unfortunately, never really performed as a club ship, as the Second World War intervened. She deteriorated during the war and was also badly vandalised and was broken up. The club then met for a while in the top room of the Crooked Billet until, in 1948, the Essex Yacht Club quit the old railway station which has been the LSC clubhouse ever since. It had ceased to be a station in the 1930s but even in my time, elderly people used to come in seeking train tickets!

Simon and I were sixteen when we joined the club and were classed, like all members under twenty-one, as cadets, paying a reduced subscription and with less privileges than the older members. Very soon after we joined, there was a meeting called of all cadets with a view to

Thames Estuary One Design 'Ernember' (TE50)

Leigh Sailing Club collection

Essex One Designs racing

revitalising their section and its activities. After electing a cadet captain as leader, we agreed to do this, with particular emphasis on the sailing side. This was not an easy aim. At that time there were no plywood or fibreglass boats and all boats owned by club members were kept on moorings. There was no central meeting point where helmsmen could be approached for crewing jobs, other than the bar, which was officially barred to those under eighteen. It was, then, impossible for cadets to consider buying boats of their own. Financially, it was also out of the question.

However there were ways and means of getting a sail, the most favoured method needed an afternoon tide. In those days it was possible to walk out over the mud during the morning to the group of moorings occupied by the club's premier class of boats, the Thames Estuary One Designs. If, as was often the case, one or more owners were scrubbing their boats' bottoms ready for the afternoon's race or doing sundry other small jobs, then a resourceful cadet could offer to help them. Once the offer had been accepted, the cadet could enquire whether a crew was needed, if not on the boat being worked on, perhaps in one of the others? This invariably worked but needed reasonable weather and the presence of at least one boat owner.

The Thames Estuary One Design was an 18ft clinker built, Bermudan rigged, half-decked boat, very similar to the Essex One Design sailed by neighbouring Essex Yacht Club. There were however a number of subtle differences. TEOD's set a spinnaker while EODs relied on a device for booming the jib round when sailing before the wind. Backstays, too, were different with TEODs operating theirs on slides running on tracks while the other class used a lever system. There were also differences in cockpit layout and in ballasting. The EOD was generally reckoned to be the faster boat, although TEOD owners were continually seeking to disprove this. Essex One Designs were also sailed at Margate while competition in Thames Estuaries was purely local with Leigh Sailing Club, Alexandra Yacht Club (Southend) and Thames Estuary Yacht Club (Westcliff) all running fleets of which Leigh was the biggest with about a dozen boats.

As though this situation wasn't complicated enough, there were differences within the TEOD fleet. A revised design had recently appeared with no spinnaker, one fixed backstay and, I believe a bigger headsail to compensate for the lack of spinnaker. One such was Berron, a boat on which I crewed several times. Unfortunately her owner was somewhat excitable and could be rather scathing when the boat did not do well. However others of this variation did do very well, notably Black Joke of the Alexandra Yacht Club.

The star of the Leigh TEOD fleet at that time was Roy Petrie in White Heather, TE 28. He had only one serious rival, Alan 'Sally' Setford, who, although a Leigh-on-Sea Sailing Club member, was sailing Santuzza, TE 33, for a Thames Estuary YC owner. Roy was the type of person who could get away with things. For example, I can remember him saying to a lady crew member: "Just keep your eye on that barge over there and let me know when he drops his topsail" and then calmly relieved himself over the stern while she was engrossed in this task!

My first race with Roy was from Leigh to Benfleet. In those days such events were not taken too seriously and the whole thing was looked upon as an excuse to drink the Benfleet Yacht Club's beer, especially by Roy. So we sailed to Benfleet with five on board – Roy, myself and another official crew member and the girlfriends of two other TEOD helmsmen as passengers. We were first to arrive at Benfleet, thereby achieving Roy's objective of maximum beer drinking time. Possibly the weight of five persons on White Heather had something to do with this as it was blowing quite hard.

What did surprise me, as an impressionable young cadet, was the amount of bad language Roy used with two young ladies aboard. But, as I have said, he was the sort of person to get away with it and, in any case, this was long before political correctness. I think that I can fairly say that, in my formative sailing years, I crewed upon most of the Leigh TEOD fleet, but it was from Roy that I learnt the most and had the most fun with.

Of course there were other ways a cadet could get a sail. During the school holidays it was possible to make contact with several retired club members who were only too pleased to have company on a mid-week sail. One such was Bert May, who sang continually while sailing. There were occasions when one of the TEOD helmsmen would be on holiday and fancy a sail. Then there was Sid and Ted. These two were East Enders, who between them owned a great variety of craft over the years and were often looking for crews. Both were bachelors at the time and would descend on Leigh on either Friday or Saturday for a week-end of sailing and drinking. They would both stay in lodgings conveniently near the club and were the best of friends although they would spend a lot of each weekend squabbling and striking sparks off one another.

Ted was quite a good helmsman and a pleasure to crew for but Sid, on the other hand, was 'interesting'. He owned a succession of boats that were past their prime but always tried hard despite the handicap of poor eyesight. The boat that he owned when I first crewed for him was Alcid, a Bermudan rigged vessel that had a fixed rudder, a distinct disadvantage in the shallow waters of the Thames Estuary. Since Sid would never give up a race until the tide was well on the ebb, he and his crews spent much time lifting Alcid off various local mud banks. We cadets learnt a lot from Sid, even if it often came under the heading 'how not to do it'.

Sid's usual sailing garb was long khaki shorts, wellington boots, an old shirt and a pullover that was more holes than anything else. Add thick pebble glasses and a pipe clenched between false teeth and you

33

have the complete picture. And it took a lot to change Sid's appearance. Leigh Sailing Club often had cruiser races that finished at the Medway Yacht Club. Many of those involved would have dinner at the club in the evening, for which they were expected to wear at least blazer and flannels. One crew, comprised of former bank managers dressed up for the dinner on a regular basis and were then delicately transferred to shore by the Medway Club's launch. Just outside the clubhouse was a tap, normally used for filling water containers and here, on this occasion, the bank managers encountered Sid stripped to his vest and scrubbing his false teeth under the tap.

"Goin' in for a pint?" he hailed them, "I'll be in later." They shuddered.

I suspect that some of Sid's outlandish behaviour was deliberate for he could not stand pomposity. One particularly upright member of Leigh Sailing Club was spending a weekend with friends on board the sailing barge that they had made their home. Early on the Sunday morning he was sitting on the barge's main hatch revelling in the odours of breakfast cooking below when a small sailing cruiser came up the creek under power. Sid was sitting on deck, for at the time he was boatless and had secured a regular crewing job on the cruiser. As the boat drew level with the barge, he shouted: "Whatcha Fred! Had a smashing time last night! I spewed up! Bright yellow it was!" Needless to say, Fred didn't fancy his breakfast after that.

In between sailing and drinking, time hung on the hands of Ted and Sid and tideless afternoons were often spent with the cadets in the club-house. We would borrow the club's dominoes and playing cards and the older men would introduce the youngsters to the delights of dominoes and cribbage. This was interspersed with occupying the Beach Café opposite the club for hours at a time and consuming numerous cups of tea. In winter, Ted would disappear back to the comfort of his London lodgings, but Sid would still visit, partly because he inevitably had a lot of work to do his current boat and partly because he also enjoyed the social side of the club.

Cadets had their own series of races with a cup or trophy presented for each one plus an overall prize. These were hotly contested as far as possible for in order to compete it was first necessary to beg, borrow or purloin a boat. Fortunately there were several boat owners, including Sid and Ted, who were willing to make their boats available, provided they crewed to keep an eye on their property. One race was in TEODs only and this was probably the best test as all competing boats were alike and handicaps were not used.

It was also possible for cadets to obtain crewing berths in the cruiser class, which consisted of those boats with accommodation, capable of sailing to ports at a distance and staying overnight. Most of this brand of racing was to Queenborough and Harty Ferry on the River Swale and to Stangate Creek and Upnor on the Medway. Under most conditions it was a more leisurely type of sailing and was renowned for the good companionship and beer encountered after the race.

One early race that I sailed in was to Harty Ferry in a small cruiser called Lilongo with the young couple who owned her, John and Joyce Raven, and Roy Petrie, of TEOD fame, who had been brought in as racing helmsman. The race started from the Ray off Leigh-on-Sea and then proceeded in a southeast direction towards the eastern end of the Isle of Sheppey. This, with a south-westerly wind, was an easy sail although the wind was freshening all the time. We were probably lulled into a false sense of security, for when we eventually hardened up to beat against the wind into the East Swale, it was quite something. Shortly after this we broke a stay, fortunately without losing the mast overboard.

Roy managed to lash the stay, which had broken where it joined the fitting that held it to the deck, but the boat was obviously no longer in a fit sailing condition, so we dropped the sails and began to motor in to Harty Ferry against a very rough sea. Fortunately the tide had turned in our favour, but before very long the engine coughed into silence. We anchored and Roy and the owner investigated the cause of the break- down. They came to the conclusion that it was a blocked fuel line, not an easy thing to fix in the rough sea that was running. The owner suggested we summon help from the shore, presumably in the shape of a lifeboat. But Roy would have none of this and quietly proceeded to cure the blockage,

With the engine running again, we raised the anchor and continued into Harty Ferry where the other boats in the race were already at anchor. A hail from one of them advised us that Harty was not going to be a very good anchorage in this weather and that everybody was moving upriver to where the Queensferry Bridge crossed the River Swale.

Here there was a small pub run by two old ladies and not much else. Still the place had the advantages of a sheltered anchorage and a supply of beer and we could convince the bridge-keeper that he was going to open the bridge for us early in the morning so that we could get back on the tide.

The pub was obviously not geared up for a large gathering on a Saturday night, and possibly not at any other times either. Its only normal customers could only have been local watermen plus the odd passing motorist. Service was through a hatch that the two old ladies kept tightly shut until someone wished to be served. They seemed utterly dismayed to have thirty or more customers and it was not long before we drank them completely out of bitter. Thereafter we drank other things and towards the end of the evening a singsong started up. The serving hatch promptly flew open and one of the old ladies proclaimed: "We ain't got a singing licence!"

Still we lasted until closing time when a party set off to bribe the bridge-keeper with bottles of light ale. The rest of us went down to collect our dinghies from the foreshore where one individual captured a large crab which he put in his oilskin pocket "because it might be important later." Owing to the shortage of space on Lilongo, I was sleeping on the Commodore's boat, a very comfortable vessel, on which I had a good night's sleep followed by a full English breakfast. After that I returned to Lilongo and sailed back to Leigh in a wind that barely filled the sails, very different to the previous day's weather.

One frequent activity for Leigh-on-sea Sailing Club was a 'Ray Day'. More or less by mutual consent, members would look at both weather and tide and decide that they should take their boats out to the offshore channel for the day. At that time most members' boats were fairly robust, being constructed of wood rather than fibreglass and could withstand the odd knock sustained out in the Ray. So, provided the weather held up, we could spend a pleasant day sailing one another's boats, swimming, eating, walking on the sands and, if feeling particularly energetic, playing rounders or cricket. Some times these sports tended to get out of hand and one or two minor injuries resulted.

'Islander' in the Ray with T.E.O.D.s astern

Dent family collection

Certain club races were scheduled to finish in the Ray, having started from the normal start line early in the morning and taken the competitors round a selection of river buoys. On such occasions Islander acted as committee boat, carrying the race officers and their equipment so that the event could be accurately finished. She tended to become the headquarters for club members for the day and was often to be seen with about four TEODs tied astern. How my mother coped with the huge demand for cups of tea, I do not know.

The club had an extensive social programme and cadets were expected to assist with this by acting as waiters for 'in house' dinners and as doorman for dances held in local hotels. This, although somewhat onerous, had its advantages, as those cadets involved received either a free ticket or a free meal. Although there was a 'fitting out' dinner and a 'laying up' dinner held in the clubhouse at the beginning and end of each sailing season, the event which all male cadets wanted to wait on table for was the 'stag' or men-only supper. Most of the club's male members, at that time, had served in the forces during the war or had at least done their National Service and knew all the cruder forces' songs. Once the supper had been cleared away a sing-song would start up and we cadets, whilst slowly stowing away crockery and so on, would be straining our ears to pick up the words. With any sort of luck our presence would be forgotten and we would remain for most of the evening. Afterwards we would piece together what we had heard and would be able to regale the other cadets with a more or less accurate version of these bawdy songs.

With Islander the hub of Ray Days, my father began recording them on ciné film and it was not long before this was extended to other club events. Indeed the filming became quite elaborate, with club members actually being required to 'act' parts and cartoons added at appropriate points. All of this culminated in the annual film show when my father and others displayed the year's filmmaking. This event was a 'sell out' with every place taken and those who did not get there early were unlucky.

The club bar was open every evening plus Saturday and Sunday lunchtime. It was manned entirely by amateurs and a roster was maintained for duty bar stewards. Like most rosters, this did not work too well as those concerned often found that they could not make it at the last minute. Les, one of the regular users of the bar, would nearly always stand in for absentees and open up for those who did not have keys. Simon and I became so used to seeing Les behind the bar that we assumed he was the steward, an illusion that he soon dispelled in his usual forthright manner.

Another regular inhabitant was Bert, a senior steward on British Railways, who weighed about 22-stone. He was normally employed on trains that connected with the Larne-Stranraer ferries and had a fund of stories about Irish emigrants coming off the ferries. He once caught one trying to light a cigarette from a light bulb – evidently he had never seen such a thing before! Bert was good at his job and was sometimes asked for by Sir Winston Churchill if he was making a train journey of any length. Apparently they hated one another but Sir Winston knew good service when he encountered it.

Bert was good fun and one night accepted a bet to swing off the lintel of the bar door. He did this successfully but his trousers flew off in full view of the ladies in the club saloon!

Leigh-on-Sea Sailing Club frequently 'played away' with team races against all the other local clubs and Burnham Sailing Club on the River Crouch. However the main 'away' events were the annual match against the Norwich Frostbites Club and Burnham Week.

The Norwich Frostbite fixture started shortly after I joined the club and I took part in the very first of these matches. The Frostbites is a club that only functions in winter and its members do their summer sailing with other clubs in the area. Their clubhouse and sailing area is at Norwich Thorpe, just below the city, where warm water from a power station keeps the river relatively free of ice in hard weather. With virtually no tide the Frostbites are able to hold a series of races each Sunday, some of which are team races against visiting clubs. When the prospect of Leigh Sailing Club competing against the Frostbites was first suggested it was decided that we would visit them one year and that they would visit us the following summer to race at Leigh in our boats. The host club would entertain the visitors to dinner on each occasion. This was varied in one year when I, as sailing secretary of the Leigh, took a private team to Norwich for an extra weekend, as the event had by then become extremely popular.

I was a member of the very first party to visit the Frostbites that probably set the pattern for future contests. By the time we arrived at Norwich the LSC contingent had visited various hostelries on the way by way of practice. We then met the Frostbites at our hotel before being whisked off for a superb meal at a restaurant somewhere in the Norfolk countryside. Finally we retired to the Frostbite clubhouse for a 'night-cap' – which went on for sometime. Amongst those present was a surgeon from one of the Norwich hospitals who had a surgical spirit that would turn gin blue and this kept us entertained for some time. Another source of amusement was the after effects of a curry that several of us had eaten in the buffet of Norwich station! The Leigh party returned to its hotel and kept the night porter busy with demands for beer and sandwiches. It was discovered that there was a honeymoon couple staying in the hotel and various tricks were played on them, including ordering them every Sunday paper that we could think of. All of this, plus some confusion over damaged furniture, resulted in us being banned from the hotel. But it didn't matter because we found one that suited us better for the next visit and remained with them.

The next morning a very hung-over LSC team turned out for the sailing. This was in 14ft Norfolk dinghies, clinker-built and gaff rigged, not unlike the RNSA dinghies I was to sail later on. At least two races were sailed so that all the visitors had the opportunity to take part. Whereas we visitors were restricted to those who had attended the weekend, no such limitation applied to the Frostbites and we very often found ourselves sailing against a very different group of people to those who had drunk with us the night before.

The result of the racing was, therefore, rather a foregone conclusion with the LSC team having to contend with strange boats, an unknown course and hangovers. Nevertheless the Frostbites did have some very good helmsmen among their members and probably would have won anyway.

The quay outside the Frostbite clubhouse gave a very close view of the racing and it was possible to exchange badinage with boats as they passed. On that first occasion I remember Ivan Hills, normally of the TEOD Sirius, intoning as he sailed past, last in his race: "And it is written that the last shall be first."

After the sailing we would adjourn to the clubhouse for a meal, prepared by the Frostbite ladies, and yet more beer. Then it would be time to return home, possibly finishing the weekend by visiting our own clubhouse to yarn about our exploits.

When the Frostbites visited us the weekend followed a similar pattern, although tides dictated when the sailing could take place. The Frostbites wanted to sail TEODs and were very disappointed when the demise of this class came. Nevertheless racing continued largely in GP14 dinghies and altogether competition between the two clubs lasted over fifteen years. It was eventually killed off by the reluctance of owners to lend expensive racing dinghies to strangers, however experienced.

Another big 'away' event was the annual Burnham Week, then rated second only to Cowes Week as a regatta, although the muddy estuary of the River Crouch was considered something of a disadvantage by some. Others, however, preferred the less formal atmosphere and felt that the estuary with its mud banks gave the racing added spice.

Burnham also had a reputation for high jinks. For example, on the first night of the week a 'no parking' sign would inevitably appear on the Fairway Buoy just off the town. This went on for years, and, so far as I know, no one was ever caught in the act of this prank.

Both TEODs and EODs were raced at Burnham with the latter class starting five minutes before the former. For a TEOD to beat an EOD was rare at the best of times, but to do so at Burnham with an additional five minute 'handicap' was a much sought-after achievement. It was none-the-less achieved a few times amongst much ribbing of the EOD crews.

Racing started at a civilised hour of around eleven a.m. and there was much competition among TEOD crews to finish before the Crouch Yacht Club closed its bar. This club was close to where the TEODs moored at Tucker Brown's moorings and its attraction was that bitter was served in real pewter tankards. With a fast race, a smart pack-away of sails, etc. and a prompt lift ashore from the trot boat, operated by a grumpy Essex character named Chum, the target of one or more tankards was achievable.

It was at Burnham that Roy Petrie really came into his own. He excelled both in the sailing and social life. And at Burnham he came up against his arch rival, Sally Setford. I crewed for both of them there and, although Roy was the better fun to be with, both were experts in the guile needed to sail in the narrow rivers Crouch and Roach, both well fringed with mud banks.

One particular race with Petrie in White Heather stands out. It was typical Burnham weather – sunny, with a fresh north-easterly breeze. The tide was flooding and therefore both wind and tide would be against us on the first, down-river leg, which would mean that progress would be slow, with short tacking against wind and tide, trying to stay out of the tide as far as possible and with the chance of going aground at the end of each inshore tack. Naturally all the other boats in the fleet would be doing the same thing and there would be plenty of calls of "Starboard!" from boats on the right-of-way tack and "Water!" from those in danger of being put aground.

We, in White Heather, spent some considerable time duelling with a boat from the Alexandra YC, with the two helmsmen constantly calling "Water!" and "Starboard!" Eventually Roy had had enough.

"I'll fix this bugger," he muttered to the crew.

All of a sudden he let out a tremendous bellow of "Starboard!"

although White Heather was on port tack. The other boat, by then thoroughly confused, tacked and Roy sailed past her, ready to take on the next opponent.

There was an official social side to Burnham Week – dinners, balls, etc. – but this was generally thought to be too expensive by the LSC contingent and, indeed, by most of the centreboard boat sailors present. For us a typical evening's entertainment would be a pub-crawl finishing in the back bar of the Royal Burnham Yacht Club, which was for men only and was apt to stay open until the small hours. Lomax, an imperturbable steward who only drank Coca-Cola, invariably manned the bar and, while proceedings tended to become rowdy at times, Lomax was always unmoved.

Burnham Week, then staged in early September, was always the end of the yachting season at Burnham, but not at Leigh where we continued until October. The boats were then laid up for the winter, either on the sea front or on Victoria Wharf, opposite the clubhouse. This was a time of great excitement, for the heavier vessels had to be lifted out by crane, often at the limit of its capacity with a party of club members clinging to one end of it as a counterweight.

Sailing barge 'Memory'

Author's collection

During these early years at the club I kept up my interest in the Thames sailing barge. Pure sailing barges were, by now, becoming rare and it was, for me, an exciting event to see one waiting in the Ray for a local pilot or huffler. Memory and Verona were two that visited with timber but both were towed in.

Bell Wharf closed during this period but there was still traffic to Theobald's Wharf, ballast being the alternative to timber as a cargo. What must have been a sudden demand for ballast led to all the sailing barges of Francis & Gilders of Colchester, Kitty, George Smeed, Mirosa and Centaur delivering cargoes. Shortly afterwards they were all sold off to become timber lighters. Similarly a group of barges owned by Horlocks of Mistley – Xylonite and Portlight among them – also brought cargoes.

But usually ballast was a steady trade with a number of auxiliary powered barges taking it in turn to deliver on a regular basis. These included British Empire (Francis & Gilders), Clara (Banyard), Nellie Parker (Wakeleys), Lord Roberts (Rankin, the Stambridge miller) and Waterlily (Wakeleys). In 1955 Clara managed to become stranded across Leigh Creek, a feat earlier performed by the locally owned Emma in the 1930s. But, unlike Emma, Clara was found too badly damaged to continue trading and was sold to become a Sea Scout headquarters.

There was still much trade in motor barges, but the local fleet of the Leigh Building Supply Company was being sold off and the end of an era was in sight.

And it was also time for me to start work.

STARTING WORK

The careers master at my school felt that I was not cut out for an academic career and should leave education on achieving my GCEs. A nautical career was considered in the Merchant Navy, but my maths was not good enough for a navigator and, with no mechanical bent, I was not considered suitable for an engineer. That left purser or radio officer, neither of which appealed to me. Eventually the careers master came to the conclusion that I should have a job that was to do with the water without me having to actually go on it. He tried two organisations, the Port of London Authority and Lloyds of London, which I later felt should have been Lloyds Register of Shipping, since that body has more to do with ships and the sea than the insurance market.

I did not realise that the procedure for joining Lloyds included several written tests on geography, English and quick arithmetic. I therefore went into these tests more or less completely unprepared and failed them badly, especially the arithmetic. I did not get the job but at least had the consolation, after one of the interviews, of seeing the new Royal Yacht Britannia come through the Pool of London at the end of a Royal voyage. I was particularly impressed by the enthusiasm of the London lighterage trade with their tugs hooting at Britannia and crowds of lighter men and their families embarked on lighters on the lighterage roads, all waving flags and cheering. Little did I realise how my career was going to bring me into close contact with this trade for a number of years.

Although Lloyds was a failure the PLA came up trumps and in September, 1954 I reported to the dock superintendent's office, West India Dock as a junior clerical officer. This entailed travelling to Stepney East station on the London, Tilbury and Southend railway and then walking along Commercial Road and down West India Dock Road, quite a distance and I was to discover there was no direct bus link. The superintendent of West India Dock at the time and for many years to come was Mr. E. S. Tooth, a real expert on cargo handling who had written books on the subject.

Dock Superintendent's Office, West India Dock
Author's collection

Once the half a dozen junior clerical officers who were joining that day were assembled, we were ushered into the great man's presence. His office was enormous, almost as big as the outer office provided for his staff and a real coal fire burnt in the hearth. Mr. Tooth launched into his welcome address to new members of his staff. To my amazement this consisted of a dire warning not to indulge in the twin crimes of pilfering and smuggling. As though we would, I thought, we were senior members of the staff, paid a salary. We were above such things! In actual fact I found out that it was all too easy to commit a crime. If you went for a walk in your lunch hour in areas where cargo was worked, there would be plenty of spilt oranges, bananas, onions, etc. lying on the ground. If you picked one up and put it in your pocket for later consumption, you had technically committed the crime of pilferage.

Just before I joined there had been an incident where a PLA policeman had stopped and searched a man leaving the dock. In the man's pocket there had been an orange and the constable had promptly charged him. But the man was a Customs officer and next time the constable was on duty a gang of Customs men descended on his police box and searched it, finding a packet of duty free cigarettes. The constable had no knowledge of these and didn't even smoke, but still lost his job. So, although dismayed at the time, I took the warning to heart.

After Mr. Tooth had delivered his warning we were ushered back into the outer office where his staff clerk arbitrarily allocated us to offices within the dock – general office, West India Dock, general office, South West India Dock and general office, Millwall Dock. There were, as I was to discover later, several other smaller offices within the docks complex with more interesting work and a smaller number of staff, but appointment to these had to be earned and was almost looked upon as a mini-promotion, but without any increase of pay.

With a couple of others I drew general office, West India Dock, much to my relief as it was just across the road and did not entail a further walk. Here we were taken to see the person who was to be all powerful so far as we were concerned – the principal clerk, who ran the general office. These days he would be called an office manager.

The then incumbent of this position, Mr. Jeffries, was a controversial figure. After years of fighting, the staff union had just secured agreement that promotion should not be on seniority but on merit. The management's reaction had been to promote Jeffries, who was not a union member, to principal clerk and then revert to promotion on seniority, which was easier, quoting when challenged, the Jeffries case. Nevertheless, Jeffries was a good choice since he ran a very tight ship and was prepared to defend his little empire against all outsiders, even if they happened to be dock superintendent. He was good for management also, since his automatic reaction to any suggestion of overtime was "no". His bearing was such that he was the only person in the general office ever addressed as "Sir".

We youngsters received a typical gruff Jeffries welcome and were then allocated to sections within the general office. I was given export charges, which meant nothing to me, although I gathered that it was to do with 'exports'. We were then taken to meet the staff.

At the time male office staff in the port fell into three main categories. First of all there were those recruited before the war. These were now beginning to occupy the senior positions for a few years before they retired (first promotions were usually received about the age of fifty). Some of these older staff could remember the former employees of the original dock companies taken on by the PLA when it was formed in 1909, many of whom chewed tobacco and spat into a spittoon in the middle of the office. Secondly there were older men (not women) recruited since the Second World War as fully fledged clerical officers with experience of outside industry. Some of these did not last very long and I can remember one joining in the morning and resigning the same afternoon. And lastly there were those, such as myself, recruited direct from school as junior clerical officers and reckoned variously to be 'career men' or the lowest of the low.

There were also the ladies. These were brought in as women clerical assistants or as typists and expected to do much the same work as clerical officers, but for a lot less money. They received one small concession – they could go home ten minutes early to "avoid the bad language used by the dockers as they left the dock." This was rubbish as the dockers would either be working overtime or have left a lot earlier. In any case most of the women were the relatives of dockers and used the same language themselves.

I was introduced to the staff but names and personalities did not

General Office, West India Dock

Author's collection

47

register until later. I was then placed with one of the women clerical assistants who instructed me in the art of rendering export bills. Details were copied from a document known as a shipping note on to a duplicate bill pad, the words "To wharfage and porterage" being written in a panel entitled details opposite the amount. Sometime later, having written these words seemingly thousands of times, I enquired what they meant, feeling somewhat like Oliver Twist with his gruel bowl. None of my immediate colleagues knew and the question was taken up by the section leader. He eventually came back with the answer that the phrase indicated the operations performed by the PLA in handling the merchant's goods across the quay. This had to suffice and I dropped the subject.

The general office probably had not changed a great deal since it was built. The furniture still largely consisted, in the 1950s (and for a good while afterwards) of high desks that were easier to stand at than to sit at. But at least high stools had disappeared and been replaced by four-legged high chairs with a backrest. As well as export charges the main office accommodated the import ledgers, timber ledgers, the wages section and the typists. The last were not a good idea as the noise from their machines could be intrusive, especially when us lads decided to practice typing in our lunch hours, an activity guaranteed to lead to complaints from older members of the staff. A side office held the dues section and the staff clerk, with the principal clerk's office in one corner. The washroom was surprisingly spacious and had just been refurbished. At one end of the building was a lobby for lorry drivers (still referred as 'car men' from the days of horse drawn vehicles) to hand in their documents and at the other the cashier's office.

Probably the most obvious character in the export charges office was George. He lived south of the River Thames and had worked for many years in the Surrey Commercial Docks, also south of the river, and could see no reason why he should not still be there instead of this rat hole. He was definitely not happy and it showed particularly in his telephone manner. George was quite capable of picking up the phone when it rang, shouting, "Fuck off!" into it and replacing the receiver. He also professed to hate just about everybody else in the office and usually had several feuds running at the same time. One of his pet hates was Tom, one of several foremen working in the general office for health reasons. Tom's work consisted of underlining in green ink the name of the merchant prepared to accept PLA charges on each shipping note. To assist him, he had an enormous ledger of firm's addresses, so large that he had to shift his weight from one foot to the other as he consulted the pages. This had worn a groove in the lino under the desk.

Tom's work went direct to George, who was quick to spot anything not quite right. It certainly relieved the monotony, when, with a great shout of: "You've bloody well got this wrong, you silly old sod!" George would bound over to Tom's position. The ensuing row could last half an hour. Matters were further complicated by Tom's own feud with Claude, another former foreman. Claude had very definite views on any subject you cared to mention and, although his work did not bring him into conflict with either Tom or George his opinions certainly did. These conflicts were never resolved and usually the protagonists agreed to differ. Eventually Tom and Claude resolved their vendetta by not speaking to each other.

George was a great exponent of the office jacket. Most of the older members of the staff had one of these, simply an old suit or sports jacket to be worn at work to save better clothing. There seemed to be some sort of competition to have the most disreputable office jacket and they suffered all sorts of ill-treatment. Pens were wiped on them (all work was done in pen and ink, kept in inkwells) and spilt tea mopped up with them. Usually they became ragged quite quickly and, in some cases, it was said that only the patina of ink and tea was holding them together. George had one of the tattiest and therefore 'best' of these jackets.

Other sections within the general office had their characters. Import ledgers, on the other side of the office, had Jack, an avid pipe smoker who filled that side of the office with tobacco fumes. To say that Jack was an eccentric would be an understatement. True, he had been run over on Millwall Dock some years previously and this may have affected him mentally, but most of the time he was logical enough.

The main trouble with Jack was that he could not get up in the morning and received several warnings about his time keeping. He took measures to combat this, turning up one morning in a taxi, still in his pyjamas and, on another memorable occasion, sleeping in the book room in the basement, in company with the rats and mice that were its normal occupants. At the end of the day, Jack would insist that he could make up his lateness by staying late and resolutely keep working while the caretaker cleared away ledgers around. Eventually, the caretaker, who wished to go home himself, snatched Jack's work away from him which led to a terrible row. But Jack did have some endearing habits. One was the selection of a suitable tree to knock his pipe out on. He would go to considerable trouble about this, examining every tree in a road before reaching a decision. Jack ended up working in London Dock, his persistent lateness leading to the offer of the sack or the chance to try again elsewhere.

The lobby where lorry drivers presented their documents was divided from the rest of the office by a partition that did not reach the ceiling by several feet and contained several small sliding hatches, which enabled the drivers to talk to the clerks. In quiet moments we could hear the drivers conversing, grumbling or even singing in the lobby. One lunchtime the only person present on import ledgers was John, a young giant of a man, who was about 6ft 6ins tall and about eighteen stone. A lorry driver was in the lobby moaning to a colleague about "these useless clerks who sit on their bums all day, drinking tea." This monologue went on and on and eventually John, unable to stand it any longer called out: "Shut up!"

"Who said that?" demanded the driver aggressively.

John stood up and, instead of looking through the hatch, raised himself to his full height and looked over the top of the partition, down at the driver.

"I did," he intoned. The driver had nothing further to say.

At the other end of the building was the cashier's office, partitioned off from the rest of us and subject to various security measures, since there was quite a sum of money in there especially around pay day for the dockers, generally a Thursday. No one person was allowed to be in there alone and if one of the cashiers was missing then someone else was selected to take his place.

The cashier's office was alarmed with one alarm button inside and another outside, hidden under a metal plate. This was so that an outsider could summon help if both cashiers were incapacitated. Unfortunately this arrangement sometimes backfired if the plate was kicked aside and then the button inadvertently trodden on. Thus it was

50

that several large PLA policemen seized another John, a lay preacher and one of the meekest men on this earth, as he left the office. The alarm had been stepped on and the police responding to the bell that rang in the police office opposite, had assumed that John was involved in a raid.

It fell to the junior clerical officers to provide an escort for the cashier when he went to the bank, although what use a seventeen-year old and an elderly man would have if there had been real trouble, I do not know. A PLA van and driver would be provided to take us there and a variety of routes were used to throw would be robbers off the scent – all very dramatic. Except when pay-day was due, we cannot have been carrying much money and even that was probably in the shape of cheques.

Another related duty was the filling of pay packets. At the time all weekly-paid employees received cash. This was work for virtually all available hands, especially the juniors and WCAs. A pay clerk would attend from each department within the dock. These young men were the chosen few of the PLA. Selected from among the ranks of clerical officers the promotion path was relief pay clerk, pay clerk, acting traffic officer and, finally traffic officer in charge of the loading and discharge of ships. All this followed provided there were no disasters on the way. Or did it? One pay clerk at West India Dock managed to lose a case full of pay packets but still became a traffic officer, the gateway to senior management.

The system for filling pay packets followed a regular pattern. The pay clerk would be issued with the pay packets for his department and money to the value of the total of the payroll. This was broken down into notes and coins, which should exactly fill each packet with nothing left when the last one was filled. This rarely worked in practice and the session would end with pay clerks giving each other change or seeking it from the cashier. We would work in teams of three, with the pay clerk in the middle filling the pay packets and then throwing them out to each side where his subordinates (us office workers) would check them and then put a staple through them, piercing all the notes. If, at the end, there was money over or short, the whole lot had to be rechecked which entailed removing the staples. What a lot of work the computer has saved!

Unfortunately by the time I arrived at West India Dock the Great Millwall Dock Beer Riots were over, but I heard the stories, mainly from the supervisor of the berth concerned. Just after the war, when Danish lager started to be brewed again, large shipments of this beer were brought into Millwall Dock, which is part of the West India Dock complex. At that time, Millwall Dock was a proper rabbit warren of a place with many small warehouses probably dating back to when the docks were built, ideal for all sorts of nefarious practices.

The supervisor had to provide quay gangs of eight dockers for each hold of the ship that brought in the lager – probably five in total. This was usually the case in the morning but in the afternoon he was lucky if he could muster one complete gang by using the few teetotallers and any others who could actually stand upright. The rest of the labour force would be laid out in rows in the warehouse usually after fighting each other to a standstill. In addition to the lager that disappeared down dockers' throats, complete lorry loads of it were going missing, the thieves no doubt aided by the archaic lay-out of the docks. In the end the shipping company removed the lager ships to the Pool of London, where the dockers were marginally more honest and could be better supervised.

The PLA had, by law, to provide canteens for its entire staff and labour. These were tucked away in a number of places and were not exactly homes of culinary excellence. In fact quite a lot of staff preferred not to eat in them, bringing in their own food or, like Tom in export charges, walking some distance to eat in a café outside the dock. Our nearest canteen was over the dock superintendent's office and was controlled by a dragon of a chief cook. Although lunchtime began at twelve o'clock for most staff, she could open the shutters at any time up to twenty past twelve. When taken to task about this, she protested that she had to cook the superintendent's dinner first. Mr. Tooth was having steak on that occasion and several people asked whether they could have it too, whereupon she threatened to close the canteen. There was no choice of main course and Friday was always fish day. Then a choice (usually sausages) was available provided if it was booked the previous Tuesday. If you happened to be absent that day then it was bad luck.

We juniors had a particular involvement with catering – we had to take it in turn, a week at a time, to sell the tickets for meals. Armed with rolls of tickets and a float of change, the duty junior would station himself at a desk just in the entrance to the canteen and nobody was to get past without purchasing a ticket. In return for this and for accounting for the money afterwards we received a free meal, worth, in those days a shilling. It was while on duty at the canteen I noticed a peculiar phenomenon. Certain members of the staff arrived for their meal very late but I had seen them enter the dock superintendent's office below much earlier. At first I thought that they were going in there for a discussion about the work. But it was the same people and it happened almost every day of the week.

Eventually someone told me the answer and this was my introduction to that admirable docks habit – the beer cupboard. Tucked away under the dock superintendent's office was a small bar, known as the beer cupboard, the name dating back to when drinks were kept in a cupboard. Technically illegal, similar bars were hidden all over the docks system and it was basically a good idea as it was difficult in some parts of the docks to reach a pub in the lunch hour. The one at the dock superintendent's office was popular as one could meet all the top brass in there. Later a colleague told me that he felt that he had purchased his first promotion in there by buying drinks regularly for all the important men in the dock.

One feature of West India Docks was the large queues of lorries waiting to offload export cargo. These became entangled with each other and with the PLA railway system, which was still steam driven and ran on rails laid along the roads with no protecting barriers. Moreover there were rumours of bribes being offered and accepted for lorries to 'jump the queue'. Much of this chaos was caused by the large amount of cargo being shipped to the Middle East, where many new oil refineries were being constructed.

A lot of this trade went in Strick Line vessels from M Shed, Millwall Docks and it was not unusual for thousands of tons of cargo to be 'shut out' from one ship to go in next one in a few days' time.

Something had to be done to alleviate this chaos and the PLA set up a reception depot where, for a small extra fee, a merchant could leave a consignment of export cargo for delivery to the berth later on. I had moved on from writing "to wharfage and porterage" and the rendering of charges for the reception depot became one of my tasks. Unfortunately the depot was little used. Whether this was because of poor publicity, or because it was not trusted or drivers and merchants preferred the other chaotic system, I do not know, but I had plenty else to do.

Towards the end of our time as juniors, we youngsters had to attend a series of lectures at head office in Trinity Square, London, which culminated in an exam which determined our seniority as fully-fledged clerical officers, class II and, more importantly, carried cash prizes for the top three entrants. The lectures covered, as far as I can remember, English, book-keeping, geography and the history and procedures of the Port of London. Most looked upon the course as a break from work and, with a weak lecturer, who was often called away to see to his regular job, most of the time was spent larking about. Much to my surprise, I came joint second in the exam, receiving the magnificent prize of £7.50. The young man who came first ended up as managing director, while both of us who came second later took voluntary severance as 'middle management'.

As a clerical officer, I moved on to better things within export charges, or so I was led to believe. These included phoning head office with queries. I was told that the contacts at head office were very senior people and should always be addressed as 'Sir'. Eventually one of them could stand this no longer and admitted that he was a clerical officer of my own age, while his colleagues were not a great deal different. After that it was Christian names. I also stood in for the correspondence clerk, recording all letters and making sure they went to the person that could answer them. But best of all, I took over as officer in charge of filing, sorting shipping notes into numerical order within ship and making up a folder for each ship. Soul destroying work and, on the whole, I preferred writing 'To wharfage and porterage'. But never mind, National Service was not far away.

Traditionally, the PLA staff had gone into the Port Operating Group of the Royal Engineers, which loaded and discharged ships in time of war. Roughly, the salaried staff supplied the officers, foremen the NCOs and dockers the other ranks. The PLA's current operating manager had become a colonel in this group during the war and keenly promoted it, interviewing all the Authority's young men as they approached call-up for National Service to persuade them to join the group, which was put forward as a good career move.

But I had been, for some time, a member of the RNVWR and was determined to join the Navy. On the appointed day, I reported to head office for my interview with the colonel. In the foyer of the great man's office I met another interviewee who told me that he was a firemen on a PLA railway engine and was dreading his National Service but had no idea what branch he should join. He went in for his interview and, a few minutes later, emerged grinning and told me that the colonel was recommending him for Port Operating. Then it was my turn.

The colonel did not give me a chance, launching into praise of the Port Operating Group and Royal Engineers in general, as soon as I was seated. Unable to interrupt, I let him finish his diatribe.

"Well, Dent, what do you think?" he barked at the end.

Timorously, I admitted my membership of the RNVWR, and said that it was inevitable that I would go into the Navy. There was an expectant silence.

"Well done!" the Colonel burst out., "Can't beat a volunteer. Better than ten pressed men, what!" But I could detect a tinge of disappointment in his voice.

Once I returned to West India Dock, the news that I would be joining the Royal Navy was out. A number of jokes about 'the golden rivet' were made. In my innocence, I had no idea, at first, what this was, although I eventually worked it out.

For the benefit of the reader, I quote from Surgeon Commander Rick Jolly's excellent dictionary of naval slang 'Jackspeak':

Golden Rivet: Non-existent final gift from a warship's builder, supposedly fixed somewhere into the keel in order to mark the end of her construction. Any invitation to enter a darkened compartment down below to inspect this legendary feature should be treated with considerable caution.

NAVAL TRAINING

Sometime after my eighteenth birthday, I knew that I would be called up for National Service. Neither the Army nor RAF had any appeal; there was only one service for me and that was the Royal Navy and to make sure of joining it, I decided, at the early age of sixteen to join the Royal Navy Volunteer Reserve. There was one big snag, the nearest branch was in London. However, if I was prepared to train as a telegraphist, there was a unit of the Royal Navy Volunteer Wireless Reserve in nearby Westcliff. So, once a week, I cycled to Westcliff to practise my Morse and learn how to use a typewriter.

The big event of these evenings was 'stand easy' when we would break for a cup of tea, a sticky bun and a yarn. Most of the Reservists were World War Two veterans still keeping their knowledge up to date and I probably learnt more from them about the Navy life than I learnt about Morse from the formal lessons. There were also weekend exercises, but since they were not compulsory and would have interfered with sailing, I avoided them.

However, I could not avoid the fortnight's training at the Signal School at St. Budeaux, near Plymouth. We stayed at HMS Drake, Plymouth Naval Barracks and travelled to St. Budeaux by boat each day. Unfortunately, I was still sixteen at the time, and therefore a 'boy' in the Navy's eyes. Accordingly I was placed in a boys' mess and had to suffer the harsh regime imposed there. Lights out was at some impossibly early hour but we amused ourselves by holding discussions, usually of a sexual nature, in the dark. One night the duty petty officer crept in, heard one of the boys swear and promptly took him to the bathroom to literally scrub his mouth out with soap. The boys' Mess included some lads who had joined the Pay and Secretariat Branch. At that time members of that branch wore fore and aft rig, that is a suit with collar, tie and peaked hat. Some of the boys came from farming areas and had never even seen a collar and tie let alone put them on. I became much in demand as an instructor in how to wear these items.

It was a relief to get to St. Budeaux for lectures and Morse practice. Lectures and so forth were always preceded by a roll call, conducted by a chief or petty officer, who we were instructed to call 'Sir'. One day, a leading hand took the call, as no one else was available and gave me my introduction to naval humour. He was not very far into the call when an individual, not me, replied to his name with "Present, Sir!"

"Sir, arseholes," said the leading hand, without looking up and called the next name.

We had to do some actual work as well as attending lectures, etc. and I drew the job of tidying up the petty officers' Mess after lunchtime, including wiping over the tables. I was mystified by some rings of what appeared to be melted plastic, which were extremely hard to remove from the Formica surfaces. Eventually I asked the mess man what caused them.

"Why, rum, o' course," he said. The petty officers were given their daily tot of rum, which was neat, in plastic tumblers. Inevitably small amounts of rum were spilt and were strong enough to melt some plastic from the bottom of the glasses. This was my first introduction to Navy rum or 'bubbly'.

Back at Westcliff, I had to take a Morse test before being accepted into the Navy as an ordinary telegraphist for National Service. Unfortunately my result was borderline. The kindly chief petty officer telegraphist, who was our instructor, was prepared to count it as a pass, but had to refer my case to the officer, who was very much a rules man and turned me down. However he was prepared to recommend that I still did my service in the Navy, but as an ordinary seaman.

Thus it was, in June 1956, that Ordinary Seaman Dent RNVR reported to Victoria Barracks, Portsmouth in civilian dress, for basic training. I joined a class of RNVR National Service seamen, some thirty strong. I quickly found that my companions, with the exception of only two or three, had only one ambition, to become an officer.

This had not even occurred to me or the other exceptions – as long as we did our two years in the Navy that was good enough for us. The rest included several public school boys and, indeed, one was believed to be an earl and another a viscount – it was probably only natural for them to wish for commissions. At the end of basic training they were all assessed as potential officers, but only three made the grade. The others, with long faces, had to reconcile themselves to being ordinary seamen.

The only known photo of the author (left) in naval uniform
(taken in a bar on Southsea Pier)

Author's collection

Among the non-officer candidates was a lad I felt particularly sorry for. He was, like the rest of us, nineteen years old and a builder and decorator by trade. However, at this young age he was married with a couple of children. How his family was going to manage on an allotment of his meagre National Service pay, he had no idea.

Victoria Barracks was a truly disgusting place. The accommodation could, at best, only be described as adequate. We were housed in barrack rooms, one class to a room in double tier bunks. This was standard for naval barracks at the time. But the main trouble was toilets. There were, if I remember correctly, two for each class, which was probably just about enough. But most of them did not work and were well clogged up. We frequently had to search the whole building for a usable one.

A kindly petty officer, near retirement, was placed in charge of us as instructor. He took us through the niceties of wearing and maintaining our uniforms, especially our boots. These had to shine, shine, SHINE! To this end much of our evenings were spent working on them, applying layers of warm polish with the back of a spoon and using up much of our own spit.

We were also taught the rudiments of marching, so that we could at least shuffle along as a squad. Lectures were given on subjects such as the organisation of the Navy, its history and customs. Most exciting was the talk on gas and its effects, during which we were ushered into a room filled with tear gas and then invited to take off our respirators, just to see what it was like. Most of us felt the effects for about an hour afterwards.

But the best lectures were medical. They were given by a laconic sick bay petty officer and his best saying, on the subject of cleanliness, was: "The first week you have crabs, the second week you have more crabs, the third week the crabs have got you." There was also the finger. Not only was this mentioned in the lectures but also advertised in pictures all round the barracks. These depicted the chewed-up remains of a man's finger with the caption "This man wore a ring". The moral was don't wear rings on duty, they can get caught in things, especially wire rope. This campaign made a deep impression on me and I have never worn a ring.

When we finished at Victoria Barracks we were to join (with the exception of the officer candidates) one of the two training carriers, Ocean and Theseus for detailed seamanship training. But first we were

H.M.S. Ocean
Ken Tupper collection

59

allowed an afternoon and evening 'ashore'. The majority of us, with little money, opted for food consumption, with cream cakes in the NAAFI club being the favourite. Not so the 'earl' and 'viscount'. Their girlfriends arrived with a sports car and, no doubt, plenty of money. They returned late and drunk, having wrapped the car round a tree and proceeded to be ill all over the mess deck. Strangely these events were covered up, presumably because of our departure the next day.

The two training carriers were at Rosyth in Scotland, so we literally had to travel the length of the country to join them. Rail transport officers, who made sure that we caught our rail connections and even marched us to a café in London for a meal, supervised us on this journey.

When we arrived at Rosyth, it was raining, not just ordinary rain but Scottish rain which is heavier and more penetrating than rain in the south of England or, at least, that is my impression. We were dumped on the quayside where there was no sign of any transport out to the two ships. We cowered there for some hours, gathering under the quay cranes for some protection. Eventually a motor fishing vessel turned up to convey us to the ships. It turned out to be a rough and unpleasant voyage with the rain still slanting down.

But eventually we arrived at my designated ship, HMS Ocean. There I found that, because I had not had basic seamanship training with the RNVR, I would have to join a class of regular trainees and start from the beginning. This I came to consider as a disaster. Of the entire class of 'regulars' only one was in the Navy because that was what he wanted to do. The rest were either there because the magistrate had decreed that they must go into one of the armed services or because they came from poor farming areas where the choice was farming work or the services. As a result there was, at first, a low standard of honesty in the mess. For example, if you were taking off your socks and placed one behind you, it would be gone by the time that you took the second one off. Still, when I left things were improving and I am sure that several of the class ended up responsible chief petty officers.

Also I did not care for our instructors. The principal one was a Welshman who hated the job and therefore hated us, although this may have been part of his act. There was also a gunnery instructor (the Navy equivalent of a drill sergeant). If he addressed you as "Sunshine" you knew you were in trouble. This gentleman gave myself and one other extra rifle drill one evening after we had had our smallpox inoculations. I now think that this may have been to take our minds off the 'jabs' but he was not popular at the time.

In her training role Ocean had ceased to be an aircraft carrier. The hangar deck where aircraft would normally have been stowed had been converted to accommodation for the trainees but the aircraft lifts were still operational and were used occasionally to shift heavy items of equipment. Since the lift wells were often used as makeshift classrooms, there were strict instructions about checking whether they were in use before moving the lifts.

One day my class was in a lift well listening to our instructor demonstrating anchor and cable work with the aid of a ship model. Suddenly the warning bell for the lift started up and, looking up, we could see the lift slowly coming down towards us. Without waiting for instructions we each grabbed a chair and got out quick. Then some brave souls went back and helped the instructor with the ship model. The lift did, in fact, stop before it would have done any damage but there was certainly an inquiry afterwards.

Ocean and Theseus went south from Rosyth to make courtesy visits to towns in the north-east of England. When Ocean arrived at her port, we were told that we would be allowed shore leave. The main entertainment laid on for trainees was a visit to the local United Services Club, which included vouchers for free beer. There was also a dance at a hall at the back of the town, but this was for ship's company ratings only. So most of us opted for the United Services.

A bus was arranged to take us to and from the club and we arrived there in good order, only to find that the clientele consisted mainly of very old men who claimed to be naval veterans and who only had one immediate aim in life – to part us by fair means or foul from our free beer vouchers. After a while the cabaret was announced and a heavily painted woman mounted the stage and began to sing very loudly and very badly. At this point most of us decided that we had had enough and that we should try the dance. It was felt that it would not be noticed that we were trainees and not part of the ship's company.

So the bus driver, after a certain amount of bribery, was persuaded to take us to the dance. It was an interesting journey with several of the brighter sparks performing acrobatics on the conductor's platform. Meanwhile rumours circulated of the large number of girls who would be at the dance. When we entered the dance hall, without difficulty, this certainly proved to be true. The entire young female population of the surrounding district seemed to have turned out and it was difficult to spot a sailor among them. They stood around in groups talking and giggling and we had an infinite choice of dancing partners.

Spying a particularly pretty girl in a group nearby, I gave my cap to my companion, Ordinary Seaman Wiggins, known as Wiggy, a quiet steady lad from Norfolk, and asked her for a dance. One dance led to another, and then another and we were getting on very well when I became aware of a complete absence of sailors. The clock said five to midnight and the last boat back to the ship left the quay at midnight! I hurriedly said goodnight to the girl and looked for Wiggy and my cap. No sign of either. I rushed from the hall straight into the arms of a patrol.

"Where's your cap?" demanded a burly able seaman.

"My mate's got it," I blurted.

"Would this be it?" he said, producing the missing item from behind his back. "Your mate left it with me. The bus is waiting round the corner, you should just catch it." I grabbed the cap and took off. "And don't be such a prat another time!" the patrolman shouted after me. I caught both bus and boat and considered myself lucky to have encountered a friendly soul and not authority in shape of a petty officer.

While we had been ashore the wind had risen considerably and we had a bumpy ride back to the ship, enlivened by the antics of the drunks and the seasick to such an extent that the warrant gunner in charge of the MFV nearly had a fit. By the time the cargo of revellers had been discharged the MFV had taken a real hammering alongside the carrier and had to be withdrawn for repairs.

The girl had told me her address but I could remember only part of it, so Wiggy and I went ashore the next afternoon and had a fruitless search for it, only enlivened by seeing a senior chief petty officer from Ocean ejected from a pub by an irate landlord with the words "Get out and don't come back!" The chief then showed his displeasure by urinating copiously outside the pub.

On the final day of the courtesy visit Ocean was open to the public.

All I can remember about this was the competition to be selected as a gangway sentry. This gave the chance to look up girls' skirts as they came down the gangway.

Ocean then met up with Theseus again and the two ships proceeded further south with Portsmouth as their ultimate destination. On the way we had evolutions. These can consist of anything that will exercise the crew in their seamanship skills. Examples are 'Port watch of Theseus will rig a sheerlegs on the flight deck' or 'Chief cook of Ocean will report aboard Theseus with a fried egg.' The first is probably self-explanatory but the second is more complicated. Not only has the cook to fry the egg but the ship's seaboat has to launched and manned to convey him to the other ship.

We trainees got off lightly during evolutions. All that was required of us was that we sing the then popular song 'Davy Crockett'. A large 'hubbly-bubbly' CPO, who we had not seen before, appeared and led the singing of a very crude version of the song. To my regret, I have not heard this version since.

After the evolutions we came under attack. As an exercise, we were intercepted by aircraft and Motor Torpedo Boats that pressed home a series of mock attacks while Ocean's guns defended her. It was interesting to see an aircraft carrier use her armament.

A bit later on, off the Thames Estuary, both ships noticeably increased speed. The consensus of opinion was that the captain now wished to get to Portsmouth without delay. But when someone pointed out that we were now probably past Portsmouth, we began to wonder. Eventually there was an address by the captain over the ship's broadcast and all was made clear. President Nasser, he informed us, had annexed the Suez Canal and both ships had now been ordered to Plymouth and the probability was that they would form part of a task force to regain the canal.

Of course we were excited! We were going to war – or so we thought at the time. What we did get was a lot of hard work. It fell to us trainees to load Ocean for the Suez campaign. In this we were joined by National Servicemen from the army who reckoned that we were having a 'soft' time compared to them. A system of makeshift conveyor belts were rigged between the aircraft lifts and the stowage for the stores taken aboard. It was our task to take the boxes and crates from the conveyor belts to their stowage and, after a while this became back-breaking work. Surprisingly the contents of the containers were either beer or butter.

With one day to go before sailing, it was announced that trainees would not be going to Suez. Regulars would go to St. Vincent, the boys' training school, whilst National Servicemen would go to the battleship Vanguard which was moored in Plymouth. To my delight, I found that, for this purpose, I was once again a National Serviceman. The down side to this move was that we had just had our issue of duty-free cigarettes – one hundred each, with no chance to smoke them. We were reminded that it was an offence to take more than twenty duty frees on a transfer to shore.

The next day we were marched from Ocean to the naval barracks to await transfer to Vanguard. Most of us had our duty frees hidden somewhere – mine were in the lining of my raincoat. Just short of the dockyard gate, the column was halted and an officer jumped on to a railway truck, reminded us of the regulations and asked for any man

H.M.S. Vanguard

Ken Tupper collection

having more than twenty cigarettes to hand them over. Nobody moved and we were marched into barracks with nothing further said. The ironic part of this episode was that I didn't smoke – I only took cigarettes home to my parents, both of whom smoked at the time. If I had been caught, I would have been in trouble with the PLA as well as the Navy and this 'near miss' caused me to start smoking, the theory being that this would reduce suspicion.

Our new home, Vanguard, was very different to Ocean. She was moored in the upper reaches of Plymouth harbour alongside the decaying battleships Anson and Howe. Vanguard was herself decommissioning and had a very much-reduced ships' company. She was also used as an accommodation ship but with Suez going on the only other occupants were a Royal Marine band. Closed mess decks had been opened up for us and nearby was the barbette for one of her guns which gave quite a large open space where I for one could go for peace and quiet. To our delight Vanguard had separate dining halls which meant that we no longer ate in our mess as on Ocean.

The instructors were different too. The training officer addressed us on the first day. He was a lieutenant-commander who told us that he had been an ordinary seaman himself and progressed up the ranks to chief before getting a commission. There was nothing that he didn't know about the Navy and it was no good trying to pull the wool over his eyes, he knew all the dodges. We will have trouble with this one, we were all thinking, but he was no trouble at all, provided that we behaved ourselves.

My class instructor was another Welshman, but a very different one. Petty Officer Jones had been due to leave the Royal Navy and had arranged to join the New Zealand Navy where the pay was somewhat better. His family was going to emigrate to be with him but Suez had temporarily put an end to these plans, for he was being retained for the length of the emergency. This had probably dampened his enthusiasm, for a typical Jones lecture would begin thus: "Today's lecture is about anchors and cables but I'm sure that you would rather hear about my wartime experiences on MTBs. So let's go up on the foc'sle and pretend we're doing anchors and cables." The other National Service class also had a Welshman of similar outlook as instructor and both classes enjoyed their lectures and probably learnt more than under a more formal arrangement.

However life on Vanguard had its down side. Early in the morning we had PT. For this we had to cross over to the derelict Howe using a somewhat shaky gangway. Frosts had come early that year and added to the hazard of the crossing and early morning PT was not enjoyable in the cold. Much the same could be said of another early morning task – scrubbing Vanguard's quarterdeck. This was done in bare feet, with trousers rolled up and using long-handled scrubbers. A leading seaman would be in charge and spray water from a hose ahead of the line of scrubbers. It was noticeable that he wore sea boots and later we found that, outside of training, these were mandatory for any task involving water.

There were, of course, inspections aboard Vanguard, just as there had been aboard Ocean. One of these was an Admiral's inspection and the Marine band quartered aboard the ship was roped in to provide suitable music while the Admiral inspected the trainees. They were not happy about this, since it meant dressing up and temporarily abandoning their easy lifestyle. Still they had their revenge by breaking into a quick version of 'When the Saints Come Marching In.' during the inspection.

As time progressed, we were expected to do some actual work aboard the battleship. Since she was moored away from the shore, all supplies had to be shipped out by boat and manhandled to the appropriate storerooms, with the trainees providing the labour, since the ship's company was much reduced. Sides of beef and one hundred-weight bags of potatoes were two items that I handled and both were extremely heavy. Then, with three others, I obtained a special job which was to last a week. This was reorganising the canned goods store. With the decline in numbers aboard, this needed reducing in scope and the dear old victualling chief in charge wanted all peaches together, all pineapples, etc. To our surprise, we were left completely unsupervised in the storeroom, the victualling staff preferring to remain in the comfort of their office. We soon found that the contents of the storeroom completely consisted of canned fruit and that it was possible to open the cans with our knives. To get rid of empties we simply dropped them out of a porthole. Thereafter, for the rest of the week and driven by the perpetual hunger that afflicted National Servicemen, we consumed an average of four cans each per day. We finished the job a bit earlier than expected, possibly because we had reduced the contents of the store, and the old chief was so pleased that he announced that he wished to give us a present. He presented us each with a tin of pineapple, another of peaches and a third of pears. We felt highly embarrassed.

It was on Vanguard that I started to smoke a pipe, a vice that is still with me. I had been trying cigarettes but had not been getting on with them, largely because they had to be stubbed out in certain areas or when involved in certain tasks. I discovered that it was possible to draw the duty-free allowance partly in pipe tobacco and partly in cigarettes. So I could smoke a pipe and continue to supply my parents with cigarettes. I bought a cheap pipe in Woolworth's ashore and it was one of the best smokes I have ever had. That pipe lasted me a long time until I eventually left it in the Mascot Cinema, Westcliff, a few days before it burned down, the result of fireworks being let off not my pipe, I hasten to add.

Our training came to an end and we were all due to go our separate ways to our home depots to await drafting to ships. But first we had to have an end of training party to which the two classes invited their instructors. It was held in the top room of a pub in Plymouth, with drinks being brought up from the bar below. After a while we tired of bringing up trays of glasses and moved on to jugs to top up the existing glasses. Later still, someone had the bright idea that, since we were all drinking either bitter or scrumpy, to ask for a mixture of the two drinks in even larger containers. In several cases this had a lethal effect. I can vaguely remember being aboard the liberty boat heading back to Vanguard and then nothing until I was violently ill in the heads (toilets) sometime during the night. When coming off shore we had to fall in on the quarterdeck and march briskly for ward to collect our station card (leave card) when our name was called. I was told that I did this perfectly, which was just as well.

A day or so later, I was off to my home depot, Chatham, to await a ship.

THE BARRACK GUARD

On arrival at Royal Naval Barracks, Chatham (HMS Pembroke), I found that I had to work 'part of ship', the Navy term for doing odd jobs. So, since it was autumn, I found myself, with one other, engaged on a never-ending task of sweeping up leaves.

What a job for a sailor! One afternoon we were engrossed in this fascinating employment when we received a message requiring us to report to the seamen's regulating office. We immediately assumed that this was our draft to a ship. But no, we were told that we were being transferred to the Barrack Guard.

I had no idea what this was, but soon found out from my messmates. The Barrack Guard, they informed me, was a sort of police force for the barracks. It was run under strict discipline and required day and night attendance. It was definitely not a good posting. This was a garbled version of the truth, as I found out when I reported to the guard head-quarters in Drake block the next day.

The first person that I saw there was sitting in a doorway, wearing No. 8 working rig which ended in brown cowboy boots – definitely not Navy issue. I asked him where I could find the chief of the Barrack Guard. In a slow Texan drawl he informed that the chief was in an office at the end of the corridor behind him. I found our later this character was the Barrack Guard armourer, inevitably called Tex. He had definitely missed his vocation and should have been an American cowboy not an able seaman in the Royal Navy. It turned out he was a native of Faversham in Kent and not Texas, as he would have strangers believe.

I went along to the office at the end of the corridor not knowing quite what to expect to find there. But I was back with the Royal Navy. The occupants were an elderly chief and a youngish petty officer, both immaculately turned out and, from their badges, both the dreaded gunnery instructors. The chief, who appeared to be a kindly man, invited me to sit and commenced to tell me about the Barrack Guard, with some interjections from the petty officer who, from his accent, was yet another Welshman. The guard's duty was to guard the barracks which meant manning the gates and other key points twenty-four hours a day, seven days a week. To this end the junior ratings did watch keeping as at sea. There were four watches, two of which would be present, while the other two were on leave. The pattern was forty-eight hours on duty, then forty-eight on leave, extended to seventy-two hours at weekends (Good, I'll be able to get home more, I thought). Whilst on duty, it would be four hours on, four hours off, continuously and for watch-keeping purposes, the guard was divided into Red, Blue, Yellow and Green watches. On duty blue serge uniform (No. 3s) was worn with the addition of white belt and gaiters, police armband, a whistle and an entrenching tool handle as a truncheon.

But I need not worry about these additions, the chief went on, for my job would be assistant wardroom hall porter and for this job I would just wear No. 3s with gaiters. He added that, although there was a lieutenant-commander in charge of the guard, day to day control was in his (the chief's) hands and it was as well to stay in his good books. Somewhat mystified about the job at the wardroom, I went to the mess deck above the offices and stowed my gear in the locker provided. I was then able to go on the best part of forty-eight hours leave since my watch (Red) was not on duty.

I returned still wondering about my new job. But I did not immediately find out for it was the practice for the watch returning from leave at 0800 to turn to during the morning and clear up the mess deck. That gave me the chance to meet the other members of my watch and Tex was on hand to make the introductions. One of our number was sentry on the Wrens' barracks and had a fund of stories (probably not all true) about the sights that he had seen through open windows there.

After that, I went on duty and quickly found out about the duties of the assistant wardroom hall porter. It was not dissimilar to that of a bell-boy in a big hotel, except that the guests were all naval officers. Under the direction of the hall porter, retired Chief Petty Officer Steward, I carried luggage, issued the 'guests' with their cabin keys, answered the phone and ran messages. But there was one task that I definitely did not like – scrubbing the wardroom steps at about four in the morning to the satisfaction of the porter.

But against this, the job had several advantages. Most importantly it was possible to get some sleep during the middle of the night, either in a small guestroom provided officially for the officers and their friends or in the billiard room. But one night, I thought I was in trouble. I was curled up in the billiard room when some young officers returned from a drunken night out and began to play snooker. Fortunately they took no notice as I crept out. The stewards could always be relied on to keep the porter and his assistant supplied with tea and toast but better still there were those officers who would insist on buying the staff a drink.

This reached its peak on New Year's Eve, which the wardroom treated as a special event with a dinner and dancing. It was indicated to me that, although I was not on duty until midnight, it was well worth turning up early. I arrived about 2230 to find, crammed in to the porter's small lodge, the duty porter and his assistant, the off-duty porter and the driver of the wardroom minibus, all with glasses in their hands. They indicated the shelf where we kept drinks out of sight. On it was a line of glasses of scotch.

"Those are for you," they said. "The officers have all been buying drinks for the man who comes on duty at midnight."

I was struggling manfully with this bounty when the catholic padre of the barracks arrived. He had obviously imbibed well and had a bottle of gin with him, which he insisted on sharing with the staff. The party went on till nearly 0200. The minibus driver then had to deliver various guests to their hotels. Fortunately this was in the days before the breathalyser and, in any case, he was a Scot of the variety that can hold its liquor. When he had finished this task, the mess secretary appeared and, congratulating us all on a job well done, invited us up to his cabin for a drink. But he looked sternly at me.

"Not you," he said. "Someone's got to stay and answer the phone and I think you've had enough already."

It was while I was doing this job that I set out to return to Chatham early one morning, went to change trains at Pitsea and realised that I had left my pay book at home. A pay book acted as an identification card and was to be carried at all times.

I returned home for it, not realising, for I was still somewhat 'green' on Naval matters, that a temporary one would have issued at the barracks. Since I was going to be late anyway, I stayed at home and had a full breakfast before setting out again. By this time in the morning transport connections were not so good so I became even later, eventually arriving at the barracks at 1030 instead of 0800. At the main gate I marched boldly up to the leave window to collect my station card, fully expecting to be charged with 'late back from leave'. But the regulating petty officer merely passed the card over without comment. I can only assume that he was unaware of the Barrack Guard leave pattern and confused me with Blue watch who were not due back until 1200.

I crept up to the mess deck and changed into my blue suit and gaiters, ignoring the comments of Red watch who were cleaning up the mess deck. When I reported for duty just before twelve the chief asked: "Where have you been all morning, Dent?" So my absence had been noticed. I was about to come out with some lame excuse like having to visit the pay office but just said: "Around, chief."

He looked me straight between the eyes and went on: "You've pulled a stroke of some sort, haven't you? Well, I can't make out what it is, so you've got away with it this time but don't do it again, or I'll have you."

Shortly after this there was a great upheaval in the Barrack Guard. The chief retired and both the Welsh petty officer and Tex went to ships and the opportunity was taken to combine the job of armourer with that of Barrack Guard messenger. And I was transferred into this 'new' job. Gone were the naps at night, the tea and toast and the free drinks but there were other advantages. For a start I must have been one of the few ordinary seamen in the Navy with his own office. This was the armoury where I had a couple of easy chairs, a desk and a radio! This last was officially supplied so that I could check our stopwatch against the BBC news pips, the last one of which was supposed to be dead on the hour. In practice the radio spent most of its time tuned into Radio Luxembourg. The armoury also contained spares of the additional equipment worn by the guard – gaiters, armbands and oilskins and greatcoats that were issued when weather conditions warranted their use. Together with the messengers in the other three watches, I was responsible for the issue and maintenance of these items.

But a good half of my time would be spent in the Barrack Guard office at the end of the corridor under the close eye of authority in the shape of the new CPO and, when present, the Barrack Guard officer, Lieutenant-Commander Dove. The new chief, CPO Dixon, was awe-

71

inspiring. He was the epitome of a gunnery instructor – six feet tall, well built with a ramrod straight back. He looked, and had been in his younger days, a heavyweight boxer. And he did not suffer what he considered to be fools gladly. One of his best performances occurred when one of the ratings put in a request for compassionate leave because his wife was due to have a baby. Dixon treated him to a lecture, lasting most of the morning, on the evils of having children. Fascinated I stayed in the office and listened. "I should know I've got five of the little bastards," was a recurring phrase. Every argument the rating put up was dismissed. In the end this unfortunate said: "I suppose you're not going to recommend it, then."

"I didn't say that now did I?" Dixon retorted. "I'll put it forward to the officer. Though Gawd knows why, must be losin' me fuckin' marbles."

This may seem very pointless. But Dixon had passed an otherwise unexciting morning and justice had been seen to be done.

The new petty officer, known only as Sam, was a very different type. Elderly (for the Navy) and quite deaf, he was a bachelor and tended to mind his own business, ignoring Dixon's bluster. He was also treasurer of the instructor's bar which was in our building, but strictly for the use of chief and petty officers only. This proved useful for one very hot night Sam sent down a crate of Coca-Cola, free of charge, for the consumption of my Blue Watch opposite number and myself.

At the time we had the advantage of Jock in the Barrack Guard. He was a Glaswegian and seldom, if ever, left the barracks and was always available to do favours, like standing someone's watch for him. This was nearly always for money, but this would be waived in what he considered to be deserving cases. Jock had plenty of spare time, particularly if he was on forty-eight hours 'off'. He often used to keep me company in the armoury during the evenings and eventually I got the story from him. He had only two ambitions – to get the fortnight surrounding New Year's Eve off and to save the maximum possible amount of money towards celebrating Hogmanay. His routine was to arrive in Glasgow a few days before this event and look up his wife and kids. Then, on New Year's Eve itself, he would start drinking and know no more until waking up in police cells a few days later, when he would be informed that he had wrecked one or more pubs. He would then pay any fines imposed by the magistrates, settle for the damage with the landlords of the pubs, maybe see his family again and return to Chatham a happy man to start another cycle.

A fairly large portion of the Barrack Guard's work was ceremonial. Every day, morning and evening, there was colours. The main ceremony, involving a guard with rifles and a band, either the Marines or the Bluejackets, took place at the wardroom, but we provided the timing, hence the stopwatch and radio. The routine was for Dixon or the chief of the watch, in his absence, which was quite frequent for as he had a family in town and was strictly an eight to four man, to assemble with a Marine bugler and the Barrack Guard messenger on the patio outside Barrack Guard headquarters. The chief would position himself where he could see, between the buildings, the flag on the dockyard signal tower while the messenger, using the stopwatch, would do a countdown.

At the precise moment designated for the ceremony the messenger would shout: "Sunset (or sunrise), chief!" At this point the ensign on the dockyard signal tower would flutter down.

The chief, in turn, would shout: "Bugler, sound off!"

The bugler would sound the still, which would be heard at the wardroom, and the White Ensign there would be lowered. That was the theory, but a more common scenario was:

Messenger: "Sunset, chief!"

Silence.

Chief (under his breath) "That bloody dockyard flag ain't come down."

More silence.

Chief (still soto voce): "Bleedin' dozy dockyard signalmen. Sound off anyway!"

Bugler sounds the still.

Chief (a few minutes later): "You fucked up that stopwatch again, Dent."

"Set it by the BBC pips, chief."

"No you didn't. Too busy listenin' to bleedin' Radio Luxembourg."

This debate could last all evening, so I will leave it there.

Other ceremonies included the firing of salutes to mark the Queen's birthday. During these there was to be no movement within the

Barracks; pedestrians were to stand still and stand to attention if in uniform; vehicles should pull up. It was the Barrack Guard's duty to stop traffic on the main road just prior to a salute. The driver of the coal lorry that delivered to the barracks took violent exception to this, declaring that he had a living to earn and had no time for these silly interruptions. His language rather spoilt such occasions.

And, of course, Dixon had to go and add a ceremony of his own. For this he would summon the leading seaman in charge of the mess deck, instructing him to wear his blue suit with gaiters, etc. This was always on a Thursday, payday.

"Fancy some fun?" he would ask the killick. Of course he did, for he knew what was coming. Accompanied by the leading seaman and myself, Dixon would set out for the drill shed where the junior ratings were being paid, saying importantly to Sam: "You're in charge." Sam would immediately go back to his crossword.

At the drill shed it was my task to go round and shut all the doors bar one a small wicket door. The ratings inside were then forced to leave by this door where they would find Dixon and the killick on either side scrutinising their haircuts and confiscating the station cards of any whose hair they considered to be too long. Those concerned were told to report to the Barrack Guard office at 6p.m. with a satisfactory haircut. Then their station card would be returned. This had the effect of depriving the miscreants of a couple of hours' relaxation without any formal charge being made. As I said earlier, Dixon was strictly an eight to four man and it generally fell to me to reissue the station cards. I have been variously offered money, cigarettes, beer or violence over the time of issue of the cards.

One day Dixon called me and my Blue watch opposite number before him and proceeded to lecture us on what a lovely time we had on duty at weekends, with all the time in the world to drink tea, to eat the illicit meals that he knew we prepared, to read the Sunday papers and do the crosswords therein. Not this weekend, however, we were going to clean the office windows.

"What with, Chief?" I asked, trying to be clever. This didn't faze him for one moment.

"Why, the fluid out of the duplicating machine, o' course, prat."

So, on the Sunday morning, armed with wads of cotton waste and bottles of the magic liquid, we set about our task. The chief was certainly right; the fluid made a lovely job of the windows. But it had another effect.

"This smells like a drop of good stuff," said Terry, my companion. Rumour indicated that he was more than fond of alcohol in any form. We carried on with the windows for a while until Terry could stand it no longer.

"I'm going to try it," he said.

"Leave me out," I said, "it'll make you go blind."

Terry raised the bottle to his lips and took a deep swig.

"Ah!" he sighed, "I thought so. The real thing."

He continued to draw at the bottle of duplicating fluid until we had finished the windows. There were, of course, plenty more dire predictions of what the effect would be. As time went by and nothing happened these were amended to forecasts of medical difficulties in years to come. Some months later I met Terry in Portsmouth and he still seemed fine.

Food and drink were constant preoccupations in the Barrack Guard and also the bane of my existence. I was issued with enough tea, sugar and condensed milk to make one cup of tea for the watch going on duty at midnight. A generous stores assistant (and most of them were generous for they did not wish to fall foul of the Barrack Guard) could be relied upon to supply quite a bit extra. But this went nowhere with the continual demand for tea from the office staff and casual visitors.

The worst occasion occurred when Dixon's old ship came into the dockyard. When I went on duty it seemed that every square inch of the office contained a chief or petty officer, all demanding tea every few minutes, much of it to be made only with condensed milk, which was what they were used to onboard ship. But condensed milk was virtually unobtainable apart from the small official issue. Between making 'wets' of tea, I spent most of that watch dashing round the barracks on my official bicycle, calling in every favour I could think of in the shape of tins of condensed milk and sometimes loose tea.

Happily fresh milk did not present such a problem. Every morning I would set off on the trusty bicycle with a large Thermos slung over the handlebars. I would go to the galley in HMS Collingwood, the engineering barracks, as the cooks there were more co-operative than those at the main galley. I would ask the petty officer cook on duty to fill the flask with fresh milk and while he was doing this I would have a look round his ready-use store.

"Nice piece of bacon, Chef," I would say when he returned with the milk. He would then feel obliged to give me a few rashers and maybe some eggs, a sausage or two and a tomato to go with them. A quick call to the bakery to pick up some of the rolls just baked for the wardroom and that would be breakfast taken care of, for all these items could be cooked over an electric fire in the armoury.

One day however this cosy arrangement went wrong. There was a strange chef in the galley, who said, as soon as he saw me: "All ready for you, son," and gave me a number of packages. These proved to contain the usual 'rations', so I thought no more of it until, just as the chief of the watch and I were tucking in to our breakfast, the phone rang.

"Main gate here," said a stern voice, "Have you got our flippin' breakfast?" They obviously had a more official relationship with the cooks.

Snacks in the evening were also possible if sufficient remained from breakfast but only if they were prepared after the token evening inspection known as 'rounds'. An officer conducted these and it wouldn't do to be caught preparing illicit food by him. One evening our own officer, Lieutenant-Commander Dove, carried out rounds and once he had cleared off I set about making the evening snack for myself and the chief of the watch who I expected to call in shortly. Things were well under way when I heard footsteps go up the corridor outside. I put my head round the door to see who it was and was alarmed to find it was Dove, no doubt returned to do some paperwork.

"That smells good, Dent. What is it?" he asked over his shoulder.

"Scrambled eggs on toast with sausages on the side, sir," I replied, deciding that I could only brazen it out.

"You couldn't possibly rustle up a portion for me, could you?"

Naturally I did and when I went to collect his empty plate he said: "That was excellent. Much better than I would have got up at the ward-room." I suspect he knew about the clandestine meals all along.

Later on a friend of mine, Able Seaman Doug became the assistant butcher in the barracks. While in the Barrack Guard he had been a great consumer of tea in the office and now he offered to see me all right for meat if he could continue to call in for tea. He did this with a vengeance and gave me enough meat to feed a small army, so much so that I was forced to throw some of it away. But during this period I had one of the best breakfasts of my life – in true Australian style, four steaks with an egg on top of each one.

I have already mentioned the chiefs of the watch. They effectively acted as guard commanders, visiting each Barrack Guard post in turn day and night, ready to deal with any problems and also to help with the consumption of any food and drink available. They worked a different watch system to us junior ratings, so I was likely to see more than one of them during my watch, since they tended to settle on the Barrack Guard office when they had nothing better to do. They included some characters. There was Buck, a large and surly individual whose only generous act was to give me a jar of pigs' trotters to finish off, and Pash, whose hunger was insatiable to the extent that he would have a double helping of the illicit breakfast, then the official breakfast and then depart for home with a complete chicken in his bag. There was Michael, who hailed from Southern Ireland and liked nothing better when on leave than a good meal, a glass or two of a fine wine and the company of a handsome woman, a far cry from the usual 'pissing-up' and 'banging off' of the average sailor.

There was yet another chief, believed to have been a lay preacher, who confiscated a book that I had been given by the rating in the bedding store opposite in return for a favour. He spent most of the night reading the book before announcing: "You're not havin' this, young Dent, not a tender young lad like you, it's got women doin' it with horses an' that." To my regret I never saw the book again.

Finally there was CPO Jardine who was trying to get his service extended for the umpteenth time. He dreaded retirement since he knew no other life than the Navy. A bachelor, he came from a country district in Norfolk where the only employment was on the farms or on the buses. At his age he was unlikely to break into either job.

He was a sad figure until Betsy came into his life. Jardine loved and cherished Betsy, a small, scruffy mongrel of unknown origins who had strayed into the barracks and was adopted by him. At night she would accompany him on his rounds, a piece of rope doing duty as a lead.

When he was not on watch, he would leave the dog with the duty Barrack Guard messenger with strict instructions on feeding and exercise. Worse still, when she was on heat, she had to be kept within the confines of the office. I'm afraid that we messengers regarded Betsy as a sheer nuisance and one day she got out while on heat. We then had to throw buckets of water over her and a dachshund that had strayed into the Barracks to get them apart. This was probably how she came to be pregnant but her downfall truly came when she tangled with the Commander-in-Chief's labrador. This drew the great man's attention to the fact that there was an unauthorised dog in the Barracks and he ordered that poor Betsy be shot. Jardine took it surprisingly well.

Our other pet was a cat. He appeared one day, looking very shabby, curled up in the petty officer's in tray, probably sensing that this was a place where he could sleep undisturbed. After about three days, he woke up, cleaned himself thoroughly and took an interest in life. We gave him a good feed and he decided to stay. He remained for some weeks, including the period of the Great Cat Cull, when large numbers of spare seamen were employed to round up all the feral cats in the Barracks, which were then put down. Tommy, as we had named him, spent that period living in a locker in the armoury, much to his disgust. Shortly after surviving this event, he rewarded us by disappearing, but I did see him once more, trotting across the Parade Ground, looking more spruce than ever and well fed. He had evidently found a new and better home.

The chief form of entertainment in the barracks was the cinema. This showed a fairly recent release plus a cartoon each evening. Most of the cartoons were of Tom and Jerry and were new at the time. Word would get round "New Tom and Jerry tonight" and the result would be a full house, many leaving after the cartoon and not bothering with the main film. Some of these were worth attending, not so much for their content, but more for the repartee that accompanied them. This tended to increase in direct proportion the level of action (or lack of it) in the film and took no regard of the Wrens who were present. For example, one memorable film was a particularly uneventful romantic drama that was watched in stony silence until there was a scene where the heroine was ditching her boyfriend. A voice in the audience called out "Go on, thump her!" whereupon another wit cut in with "No! Fuck her first!"

I envied the fire engine's crew who had to attend every screening at the cinema in case of fire. They did not have to pay and I thought that watching every performance was a good perk. One of them disagreed with me though.

"Nah!" he said. "Gets bloody boring. You know the film by heart at the end of the week and it's too dark to read in the cinema."

SAILING IN THE NAVY

I had made one of my priorities on joining the Navy obtaining the Royal Navy Sailing Certificate. I did this at Portsmouth, while I was at Victoria Barracks.

I was told to meet a certain chief petty officer at the sailing centre in the Dockyard. Not knowing quite what to expect, I made my way to the centre and met the chief who explained that he was to be my examiner and, since he understood that I had already done some sailing, we would go straight out in the boat, a Royal Navy Sailing Association fourteen footer (RNSA 14). At the time these boats were sailed universally by the Navy, every ship carried at least one and groups of them were kept at each base near the water. They were clinker-built and gaff rigged and the normal crew was a helmsman and one crewmember.

The chief, who seemed a gentleman in every sense of the phrase, pointed out the dinghy that we were to sail.

"Let's rig her," he said. "You do the foresail and I'll do the main."

Once this was accomplished, he suggested a sail round the harbour. It was a lovely day with a light wind.

"You take her," said the chief once we were clear of the jetty. And so we more or less drifted around the harbour with me steering, while we consumed the beer and sandwiches that the chief had provided.

"Put her alongside," he said as we neared the jetty at the end of our sail. I did so and he jumped ashore with a line. He was gone for a couple of minutes and when he came back he handed me the coveted certificate which he had signed.

"You obviously know what you're doing," was his only comment. I never saw him again, but he must have been a yachtsman of some repute since he told me that he had sailed across the Atlantic at least twice.

The certificate entitled me to sail RNSA 14s as both helmsman and crew, including racing, but not to sail anything bigger, such as a cruising yacht. Still, it was only dinghies that I was interested in.

The opportunity to use it did not arise until I arrived at Chatham. There was a thriving sailing unit there that raced RNSA 14s, largely in team races against organisations such as the Royal Engineers and the dockyard staff. However, they did have the odd individual all-comers race. One of these was imminent and I teamed up for it with a lad I had known vaguely in the PLA. He worked in the ledger office at London Docks and I had met him on the training course for junior clerical officers. His ambition was to join the marine department of the PLA and he was eventually successful in this.

After a debate as to who should helm the boat, it was agreed that we would share it, sailing half the course each with me having first turn. We made a brilliant start, more by luck than judgment and found ourselves leading the fleet and pulling away from them. We rounded the first mark with a commanding lead but with no clue as to where the next mark was. The other helmsmen had obviously sailed the course many times before and it soon became apparent that we had sailed in entirely the wrong direction. In no time at all we went from first to a very poor last from which we eventually retired.

This experience plus the fact that the races were all of the team variety for the foreseeable future made me reconsider my position. I came to the decision that, for the time being, I would be better off sailing as a crew. But whom should I crew for? My London Dock friend had been drafted to a ship and most of the team racing helmsmen had regular crews. At this point Leading Seaman Singer arrived.

Singer had been up and down between petty officer and leading seaman several times, losing the higher position for minor crimes and then being reinstated after a period of good behaviour. He was in this position at the moment and was allocated to the Barrack Guard as the leading hand in charge of the mess deck. He was a Cockney, and certainly had a way with him, even getting the better of CPO Dixon on occasions. The following is typical Singer.

One Sunday he put his head round the armoury door and said to me and my Blue Watch relief who had drooped in for tea: "Fancy a drink, lads?"

I immediately said that I was on duty and where would we get a drink from?

"Instructors' bar, o' course, an' don't worry about bein' on duty, I'll get you covered." He disappeared for a couple of minutes.

"Right," he said, "Duty chief is 'appy to watch out for you for a while. Let's go." So we went up to the forbidden instructors' bar which was almost empty, with our petty officer, Sam serving behind the bar. He brightened as soon as he saw us.

"Ah! Lads," he said. "What are you going to have?"

The first round was on the house, the second on the mess president and the third on Sam himself. Then I had a twinge of conscience and went back to relieve the chief. Singer later told me that they had another two rounds and he and my relief hadn't had to pay for those either.

But, more importantly, Singer was a keen and competent sailor of RNSA 14s. Since he had just returned from a foreign commission, he had no current crew and was only too glad to take me on in this capacity. He was a wily and completely unflappable helmsman. On one occasion, after a race, our attention flagged and we were swept on to a moored pontoon by the tide. We were pinned against it with the boat being pushed over by the sheer force of the tide. Water poured over the gunwale.

"Rather a lot of 'aqua' in the boat," was Singer's only comment and he then set about extricating us.

Almost immediately he convinced the chief shipwright in charge of Chatham sailing that we were worthy of a place in the barracks team in the races against other teams and we had some success, although the Royal Engineers were almost impossible to beat.

The Medway Yacht Club at nearby Upnor included RNSA dinghies in their Saturday points races. A few from the dockyard and Royal Engineers used to compete but it was rare for the barracks to be represented. Singer, who rarely left Chatham since he was courting a 'clippie' on the local buses, felt that this should be remedied. He suggested to me that we take part the next time that I was on duty on a Saturday. I replied that this was all very well but I was supposed to work four hours on and four off while on duty. Singer promptly informed me that my Blue Watch opposite number, in return for a small bribe, would work six hours straight off if I would do the same later in the evening while he went to the pictures and had a drink in the NAAFI.

So, shortly after midday, we set off to take part in the Medway YC points race. The event itself was a disappointment; there were only two other competitors and the wind was light and fickle. We struggled round the course to finish third on a shortened course. Singer then suggested that we go ashore to the yacht club. Conscious of my obligation to be back on watch, I agreed but said that we had better not be long. So we sailed in and moored up to the club slipway before walking round to the clubhouse.

Since it was mid-afternoon we were disappointed, but not surprised, to find that the bar was shut. But there was a sumptuous tea laid out for competitors.

"Fill your boots," was Singer's instruction, so we both took large platefuls plus the inevitable cups of tea. When we reached the cash desk, Singer said, with authority: "Royal Navy." And this seemed to exempt us from paying. We took our tea outside and had a pleasant time eating and drinking, lying in the sun and watching the girls go by. But suddenly I realised that it was gone five o'clock. I expressed my alarm to Singer who merely said. "Don't worry, all laid on." What was laid on? I wondered, for there was now no wind at all and our base was three-quarters of a mile upstream with a strong ebb tide running.

Soon all was made clear. At about half past five a dockyard motor-boat appeared carrying, in addition to the driver, Singer's bus conductor girl friend. They towed us back to base in a few minutes. A friend of Singer's was waiting with a car to run me back to the barracks just in time to take over the watch, albeit still in my sailing clothes.

Towards the end of that summer the Command sailing championships were held at Rosyth in Scotland. Scottish Command was the host and each of the other Commands, Portsmouth, Plymouth, Fleet Air Arm and Nore, were expected to field a team. In the case of Nore Command (Chatham) this was achieved with difficulty and Singer and myself were included. The programme was to travel to Scotland on the Sunday, sail the races on Monday, Tuesday and Wednesday and travel back on Thursday. My watch pattern was that I should normally be on duty Monday and Tuesday. This would mean requesting special leave for a sporting event and a painful interview with CPO Dixon.

This entirely lived up to my expectations. First of all he asked me why I wanted to do such a daft thing as attend the Command championships. I said something about the honour of Nore Command. He then switched to boasting of his own sailing prowess, claiming to have sailed a naval cutter for miles without a rudder, and stating that when I could match this, then I could have leave. I explained that that sort of thing was up to my helmsman, Leading Seaman Singer. That did it.

"And I suppose he'll want fuckin' leave an' all!" roared the chief. "How the fuck can I run this place with all the soddin' staff on leave to take part in some daft sport?"

Nevertheless he forwarded the leave applications for both Singer and myself to our officer, Lieutenant-Commander Dove, who was only too pleased to recommend them and have two of his men in the Nore Command team.

So on the Sunday we travelled up to Rosyth Naval Base. How different from Chatham Barracks! There was a white-gaitered sentry on guard at the main gate, but there all similarity ended. On arrival we wanted two things – food and, in the case of those entitled, their daily tot of rum. It was after the normal time for supper, but while the tots were being arranged, someone offered to find a cook to dish up a meal for us.

The cook soon appeared, dressed largely in civvies and with a big tabby cat perched on his shoulder in the style of Long John Silver's parrot. He gave the impression of being very drunk, but managed to produce an excellent fry-up for the travellers.

After this we ambled round the base drawing bedding and other bits and pieces. We were then shown to a barracks hut that would be our quarters during our stay. One or two other ratings were already there and from them we learnt about the opposition for the championships. They were all National Servicemen, of the failed officer variety, and we were the only other lower deck competitors in the event, the rest all being officers. This was of interest as the Nore team consisted entirely of ratings – the chief shipwright, a CPO electrician, two Wrens, a petty officer GI, a signalman, Singer and myself.

"Good," said the ever-confident Singer. "We can show them officers a thing or two."

Next morning we were introduced to the boats. With four teams sailing at any one time, sixteen RNSA dinghies were needed which was a lot more than was normally available at Rosyth. Since the Home Fleet was in at the time, someone had the bright idea of borrowing their dinghies to make up the number. Nothing wrong with this in theory, but in practice these boats were only in good condition when their parent ship contained an officer who was keen on sailing. If this was not the case the ship's dinghy was likely to be commandeered for operations such as painting ship. Thus the quality of the boats in the championship varied enormously, as we will see.

There were no dedicated race officers to control the racing in the championship. It had been decided that, with five teams entered, we would sail with two pairs of teams racing against each other, while the fifth team acted as race officers. A draw was held to decide who did what for the first race and the Nore team drew 'race officers'.

Two drifters manned by taciturn old Scotsmen were provided as committee boats. We would work from the larger one which came supplied with suitable flags, cannons and other equipment including a dan buoy which would be laid as a limit mark for the starting line. Our gunnery instructor promptly took charge of the cannons and the signalman the flags, saying that these were their normal departments. Everybody else looking to Singer and me as the two seaman ratings to rig the dan buoy ready for dropping. Neither of us had much clue about this sort of thing but accompanied by helpful and not so helpful suggestions from the others we fiddled about with it for some time.

Eventually the wheelhouse door flew open and one of the elderly Scotsmen staggered out.

"Stand aside!" he ordered us and in no time at all he had the buoy rigged perfectly.

"Now just heave it ower the side," he told us when he had finished and retreated to his wheelhouse, muttering: "I wasna dan laying champion o' the 5th minesweepin' flotilla for nothin'."

After that our efforts at running the race went ahead with no major hitches. Then it was our turn to do some actual sailing.

This was team racing to perfection and made the efforts back at Chatham look puny. The teams sailed as teams. For example, if team A had boats in first and third positions, while the opposition had boats at second and fourth, then the leading boat was prepared to drop back and try to sail the second off his course to let the third boat take the lead at his expense while he endeavoured to hang on to second place. To achieve this type of tactic a helmsman would be quite prepared to luff a member of an opposing team right across the Firth of Forth.

I'm afraid that we did not do very well at this, either as a team or individually but we did have our moments. One of these was on the second day that promised to be a day of bright sunshine and little wind. The start was postponed and during the postponement Singer suggested that we paddle over (we at least had paddles on the boat we had drawn for that day) to the lesser of the two committee boats. Once there, he jumped aboard and, after a brief conversation with the crew disappeared down below. A few minutes later, he was back, bearing two lumps of rusty ballast and a long length of line.

"This'll be our anchor," he said, "an' that'll be somethin' the others ain't got. We'll need it in this light stuff. Don't want to get swept away by the tide."

Unfortunately for his plan, the breeze filled in and an anchor was not needed.

For the last race, sailed in a good blow, we drew one of the less well looked after boats. Soon after the start, it became obvious that the gaff jaws that held the gaff on to the mast were damaged and not doing their job. I spent most of the race standing on the main thwart, holding the jaws onto the mast, while Singer sailed the boat single-handed. This was deemed better than putting our team even further behind by retiring and, although a good last, at least we finished. It was a feat worthy of CPO Dixon.

After the last race there was a lunch and prize giving aboard the depot ship in Rosyth dockyard. Everybody concerned was still in his or her sailing clothes and it was difficult to tell officer from rating. I found myself sitting next a middle-aged man who was intrigued by the fact that the Nore team was comprised of ratings only and interested in my exploits with the gaff jaws. Later on I found out that he was an admiral. After the prizes had been presented we packed and travelled back to the south of England. I went home to complete the 48 hours off that I should have been on (A sore point with Dixon until I pointed out that if I went straight back, it would play havoc with his shift system.) Of all things I went sailing again.

I had no means of knowing it but my time at Chatham was now nearly up. But there were still a few events to happen there. The first was my twentieth birthday. On this date I was entitled to draw my tot.

All men aged over twenty could indulge in this delight, although they had the option of being classed 'Temperance' or 'T' and receiving money instead. The 'tot' for junior ratings was watered down; two parts of water to one of rum and the mixture amounted to almost half a pint. It was dished up in the foyer to the dining hall just before the first serving of lunch at twelve noon. All entitled ratings had a card that was clipped each time they drew their tot and the drink had to be consumed there and then. Much stricter than the routine onboard ship.

One day I was late arriving for my tot by some twenty minutes simply because I had been talking to someone. By this time the foyer was deserted and everyone had gone in for lunch. I was still wearing my white gaiters and as soon as the rating issuing the rum saw these, he said: "Barrack guard, you're entitled to neat rum." So I enjoyed a tot of 'neaters'. In later discussion, it became apparent that no one else in the guard had heard of the practice of issuing the guard with neat rum and it was generally assumed that the rating issuing the rum was working some kind of fiddle and didn't wish to water any more rum.

About this time there was an organisation and methods investigation into certain departments within the barracks. Chief Dixon, much to his delight, found out that one of his archenemies, the drafting master at arms, had been found to only be doing twenty-five minutes actual work per day. Let O & M come over here, I thought grimly, they'll find a chief of the Barrack Guard who manages to do even less.

Another of Dixon's enemies was the provost marshal who was responsible of the policing of the town of Chatham, while Dixon was responsible for the same operation within the barracks. This warrant officer had an unusual name and, back home at Leigh, I was interested in a young lady of the same name. One day she told me that her father was something of importance in the Navy at Chatham. Oh no! I thought, and here am I working for the opposition! End of possible romance.

I found a new friend to share some night watches with. The duty petty officer would often call, scrounge a cup of tea and whatever else might be available in the eating line. I got to know several of them quite well, but this particular one stands out. He was a gunnery instructor, but far removed from the Dixon mould. An educated man, he could discuss books, art, cinema and even ballet. This made a refreshing change for me from the normal topics of sex, football and Naval tittle-tattle. But how did such a man become a GI? He never even raised his voice, did not swear and did not even use much naval slang. Eventually, I found out.

"That man," said my informant, "is about the best brain in the gunnery department. He's a boffin. Even designed gunnery control systems. He's been offered a commission scores of times but won't even accept going up to chief. Says he prefers life where he is." Takes all sorts to make a Navy.

Towards the end of my time at Chatham, I was nearly charged under the Official Secrets Act. It came about like this. It was a quiet Sunday afternoon when suddenly the phone rang. It was the duty officer at the gunnery school who enquired whether I had a bicycle. I said that I had and he then asked me to take a package to the home of the captain of the gunnery school at his home in the town. As politely as I could, I informed him that I couldn't leave my post in case of an emergency, whereupon he told me to find someone to relieve me and carry out his order. After a short while the chief of the watch arrived and I explained the problem, hoping that he would back me. He didn't like the proposal anymore than I did, but said that orders were orders and he would stay in the office while I went into town. So I collected a package that felt like dance tickets and cycled into town.

I found the captain's house all right, but repeated ringing of the door-bell did not produce an answer, although I could hear voices inside the house, probably the captain's stewards. I did the logical thing and put the packet through the letterbox.

Next morning, all hell was let loose. The packet, it was alleged, had not arrived. I was summoned to see our officer, Lieutenant-Commander Dove, who was on the phone, presumably to the captain. He broke off the conversation and asked me for my version of events. He then picked up the phone and repeated it, adding that I was a reliable hand and that if I said I had put the packet through the letterbox then that is what had happened. And that, officially, was the end of the affair. Later, from Dixon, I heard that the officer had no right to order me away from my post and that the chief of the watch should not have condoned it. But I was to fall foul of that officer again.

About this time we acquired a new, keen commodore of the barracks.

He let it be known that he intended to exercise either a security alert or fire within a few days of taking over. A security alert would, at that time, have assumed an attack by the IRA.

What chance the Barrack Guard would have stood, armed only with pick-axe handles against a determined assault, didn't bear thinking about, so it was assumed that a fire exercise was more likely. This proved correct and, quite quickly, Dixon's spies were able to tell us the date and approximate time of the exercise, but not it's location.

The day suggested passed without incident. At four p.m. Dixon went home, as usual, exhorting the duty watches to stay on their guard. The evening went past and about 11.45, I was just thinking that the spies had got it wrong, when the phone rang.

"For exercise, for exercise. Fire at the commodore's house!" The crafty old sod! Fire at his home, he wouldn't have to move far!

I sprang into action, ringing both our fire engine and the civilian fire brigade in the town. Then I raced over to the block opposite and roused the fire picket. All seemed to go well, fire engines, pickets etc., all got there within the prescribed time and were seen to do so by the great man himself, standing on his balcony in his pyjamas and dressing gown. But after a while, it became obvious that there was a complete absence of the specialists that would be required in a fire situation, electricians, shipwrights and the like. Subsequent investigation proved that there was no requirement for them to attend, let alone have 'a shake' to wake them up.

It was probably the same commodore who decided that there was no need for a dedicated guard to perform 'colours' in the morning. Instead this duty was to be performed by the off-duty watch of the Barrack Guard. This was not a popular move. Bang went any chance of an official breakfast, terrible though these normally were, and turning to clean up our mess deck would follow the duty. Nevertheless orders were orders and my watch, Red, was to be first to be the guard. Dixon, deciding that we were probably all rusty at rifle drill, ordered us to a practice on the drill square. This was held one afternoon, again when we were off-duty and led to much moaning.

When I dropped my rifle for the second time, Dixon summoned me out the front.

"'Ow much rifle drill 'ave you done, Dent?" he growled out of the corner of his mouth.

"One afternoon, Chief," I replied, truthfully. He considered this for a moment.

"I'll do a deal with you, you..." he muttered. "You stay in the office while guard's goin' on. But when the rest of us comes back, I want a cup o' tea for each man an' I don't care 'ow yer does it. And, the night before, you clean me boots an' me medals an' they've got ter be gleamin', gleamin', gleamin'. DO YOU UNDERSTAND?"

"Yes, Chief," I replied meekly, relieved.

"NOW GET BACK IN THE RANKS, YOU STUPID PRAT!" he added for the benefit of the others. Naturally word soon got round about the National Serviceman excused guard and my popularity sunk even below that of Dixon's. But I didn't need to worry about this as my time was virtually up at Chatham.

HMS VICTORIOUS

My first intimation that I was leaving Chatham came when I returned from leave after Christmas. As I walked along the main road of the Barracks, a friend of mine, Nobby Clarke, was coming the other way.

"You've got a draft chit!" he called out as we drew level. Now I had heard this so often it was, I believed, a typical case of crying 'wolf'. By then I was confident that I was not going anywhere and would see my time out at Chatham. How this would equate with me becoming an able seaman, as I should do after eighteen months service, I did not know or care.

But when I reached the office Dixon told me, with great relish, that this time it was true. I, with several more from the guard, was due to join the aircraft carrier HMS Victorious at Portsmouth. It didn't end there for several others including Dixon, Sam, Singer, the assistant butcher, Doug and my opposite number in Blue Watch were due to go their separate ways. A vicious rumour went round that there had been a clear out of the Barrack Guard for some (unspecified) crime. But I think that in my case someone in authority had woken up to the fact that here was a National Service ordinary seaman, almost due for AB, who had never been to sea.

Shiner, a two badge AB (eight years undetected crime in the Navy) was also joining Victorious and, since he lived in one of the Medway towns, we agreed to meet at Waterloo Station and travel down to Portsmouth together.

Needless to say, we caught the last possible train from Waterloo, one leaving at midnight to give ourselves the maximum time with family and friends before embarking on this new venture. We slept as much as possible on the train and, on arrival at Portsmouth at about three in the morning, transferred to that excellent establishment, Aggie Weston's, for coffee and more sleep before reporting to the barracks.

A commissioning office had been set up for Victorious within the barracks and, although we were not expected to report to it just yet, Shiner decided to do so anyway, declining my offer to go with him.

"Leave it to me," he insisted. He returned bathed in smiles.

"All fixed," he announced. "We're in the same mess, I've got the best job on the ship an' you've got the second best."

I enquired as to the nature of these jobs. He replied that his was mess deck sweeper, looking after the cleanliness of our mess, while mine was 'vent party'. I pressed him for more detail but all he would say was: "I told you, second best job on the ship."

Victorious had been refitting for about the last seven years and had become somewhat of a joke in the Navy. Wags said that bets were being taken on whether the tugs would be able to pull her off the reef of tin cans that had built up under her when the time came for her to go to sea. She was one of the Navy's largest of aircraft carriers with a complement of around two thousand men, when fully manned with the aircraft squadrons aboard. So much for my request to serve on small ships when I first joined up!

Within a few days she was ready to take onboard those of the crew who were waiting in barracks and they were to do it in style and march through the streets of Portsmouth. This we did, harangued by strange petty officers and accompanied by a Marine band that we could hardly hear towards the tail of the column. The citizens of Portsmouth, who had seen it all many times before, took no notice of this display and

H.M.S. Victorious

Ken Tupper collection

carried on with their work or shopping.

When we arrived, we found our kit and stowed it in our mess decks. Shiner started as he was to continue, producing a cup of tea and a sandwich for all in the mess.

We then had to attend briefings about our jobs, in my case, the mysterious 'vent party'. Shiner hadn't been wrong, it was a very good job. Based on damage control headquarters (DCHQ) it consisted of wandering around the ship checking that all ventilation fans were working properly. If they were not, all we had to do was report them to DCHQ and an engineering team would take over and carry out any necessary repairs. Moreover this was also our job when duty watch, whether in harbour or at sea.

The only immediate drawback was that I was duty watch that very first night. I was told to leave the phone number of my mess with DCHQ and that they would contact me if I was needed. This seemed a sinecure until the phone call came through. Apparently there was a problem with the fans in the engine-room artificers' mess. Now where in this huge ship was that? It is possible to find your way round a warship using the compartment numbers, which do follow a pattern. DCHQ gave me the number and letter for the mess and I found my way to the approximate area where it should be. No sign. After searching for about half an hour, I followed the sound of typewriters and found myself in what appeared to be the bridge wireless office. I asked the telegraphists in there whether they knew where the ERA's mess was. No, they didn't, they replied, they had only just joined the ship.

Disgruntled, I reported back to DCHQ, only to find there had been another, angrier phone call. I checked the compartment number and set out again. Another long search still didn't reveal the mess. I decided to lay low and heard no more. I didn't find the compartment the whole time I was onboard Victorious and eventually suspected I had been the victim of a 'wind-up'.

Shortly after this the ship was due to sail and carry out a number of trials to prove that she was fit for active service. Speculation as to whether she actually leave Portsmouth grew apace. In the end, the majority opinion was that she would not, something was bound to go wrong.

My station for entering and leaving harbour was in the cable locker and the cable party assembled there ready for this momentous first departure. At the time we didn't know exactly what was required of us and had mostly been influenced by the cynics who believed that, at the end of the day Victorious would still be moored to the quay at Portsmouth. Therefore we were all dressed in the No. 8 working rig of trousers and shirt only, for, although in was January, it was quite warm below.

So we sat in the cable locker, which was quite a large compartment, smoking and yarning and listening to assorted thumps and bangs from outside that did not tell us much.

After a while a voice shouted down one of the hawse pipes: "Cable locker, can you come up and give us a hand?" We trooped up to the cable deck above to find the ship at sea, somewhere off the Isle of Wight, which was a vague blur on the horizon. It was bitterly cold on deck with a bit of spray flying about and in our inadequate clothing we were frozen. But not for long, for we were soon helping to tighten up Blake slips and other mysterious devices on the cable deck. We learnt from this and always afterwards went to the cable locker armed with jerseys and oilskins in case we had to go on deck.

Sea trials then commenced. Because the necessary facilities were in different parts of the country, these could not all be conducted in the Portsmouth area, so Victorious toured round the country, visiting the Clyde area of Scotland and Portland among others. Heeling trials, however, were conducted off the Isle of Wight. These consisted of seeing just how far the ship could lay over on her side in safety. No doubt a Naval architect had already come up with a desirable angle of heel and this was the figure that the captain sought to attain. The heeling threw up some minor weaknesses that often manifested themselves in the shape of burst water pipes. Temporarily pulled off ventilation party, I spent a lot of time helping bail out partially flooded compartments.

During the trials the crew shook down and became used to their jobs, in my case the ventilation party. Actually there was very little to do. The party consisted of four seaman ratings under a petty officer. For damage control purposes, the ship was split into four areas and these applied to ventilation also. So each rating had a part of the ship each and had to patrol it once in the morning and once in the afternoon, reporting anything that was wrong. This took about fifteen minutes each time, so there was plenty of time to spend in DCHQ, drinking tea, yarning and doing every crossword we could find in the papers, which we were not short of as they were delivered by helicopter each day.

But DCHQ could be a busy place and sometimes we had to make ourselves scarce.

We soon found that there were four unmanned damage control sub-depots. It was possible to borrow the keys to these and hide up in them for a read until things quietened down. On one occasion the crossword session was in full swing when the commander (who was second in command of the ship) entered DCHQ.

"Make yourselves scarce," muttered the petty officer, putting away the paper. Carrying our clipboards and trying to look important, us two ordinary seamen who had been with him made to leave DCHQ. But my companion was smoking.

"Chief," said the commander to the CPO in charge of DCHQ, "there is a rating about to leave this office smoking. If he does so, put him on a charge."

Smoking was permitted in offices and mess decks, but nowhere much else. All commanders, whose next step would be a ship of their own, tended to be 'holy terrors'.

The cable locker job settled down, too, for dodging in and out of harbours, we were getting plenty of practice at it. Even if anchoring was not required, we had to be in the locker in case of emergency. Anchoring was simple. The anchor was let go from the cable deck above and the chain would run out at a tremendous pace, amidst clouds of rust. While this was going on we would be crouched behind a protective crash barrier at the back of the locker. Up anchor was very different and this was where the cable locker party came into its own.

The chain would come in very slowly but relentlessly. Four of us would stand at each corner of the appropriate cable bin each armed with a rope attached to the deckhead. The theory was that each in turn would catch a bight of his rope round the cable and train it round the bin. This was dirty, hot and wet work and normal rig for it was underwear and overalls only. It was easy to get your rope trapped in the cable and when this happened we would help each other to clear the obstruction. The worst that could happen was that the leading seaman in charge would have to shout up to the cable deck for the hauling in of the cable to be stopped, while we sorted things out.

It soon became apparent that not all the cable party was needed on every occasion. So we were split into watches and even parts of watches. This was not, necessarily a good thing. Up in Scotland, where we went for some of the trials, we were all sitting round enjoying our 'stand-easy' with a cup of tea and chocolate from the NAAFI when, over the ship's broadcast, came the pipe: "First part of the port watch of the cable party report to the cable deck!" This quickly escalated to: "Port watch of the cable party to the cable deck at the rush!" I was starboard watch so I sat tight until: "Anyone from the cable party to the cable deck at the rush!" I sped away, imagining that the ship must be dragging her anchor on to rocks, although cynics felt that the captain merely wanted the ship moved so that he had more light in his cabin. We spent an interested hour or so, those of us who had got there, heaving cable in and out for a purpose that was never explained.

During the trials period we also settled domestically. My mess was a big one, containing about thirty-four seamen ratings. Although there were a few bad characters, most were reasonably pleasant. If there were arguments, they were about the sleeping arrangements. Victorious was the first major Royal Navy ship to be equipped completely with bunks instead of the traditional hammocks. But the bunks were not a fixture and a framework had to be erected each night to hold them and this could only be done after 'rounds' at nine p.m. This led to endless arguments. Firstly no one was terribly willing to undertake the chore of erecting the framework. Secondly we all had different ideas of what time was a suitable bedtime – there were those who wanted to turn in early and those who preferred to wait till official lights out. Eventually having a roster to put up the structure after rounds solved the argument and, after that, the individual could slide his bed in when he wished to retire.

The atmosphere on the messdeck was not improved by Shiner's knitting machine. He clattered and banged away on this most evenings to produce knitwear, some for his family and some for sale. But no one could really complain for, as mess deck sweeper, Shiner really looked after us. The mess was always immaculate and every day when the rest of us returned from work Shiner was ready with a cup of tea and a

Seamen's messdeck on Victorious. The author is partly obscured at the back.
Leading Seaman Ford is at the right of the front row.

Author's collection

snack – a sandwich or a cake that he had scrounged from somewhere.

Shiner was also rum bosun, a job that traditionally went to the senior member of the mess, the next senior taking on the job of recording who had had their tot. Shiner would draw the tots for all who were entitled. He would then issue these to individuals, taking care to keep his thumb in the measure to provide 'extras', for himself and his assistant when the rest were served.

One Sunday towards the end of my time on the ship, there were only about eight of us on board, of whom only five drew their rum. Shiner was amongst those present, but I was the next senior man, having just been promoted to able seaman, so I was the assistant on that occasion.

Shiner came back from drawing the rum looking worried and took me to one side. He explained that he seemed to have been issued with rum for the whole twenty-something who normally drew their tot. What should we do? I gave the answer I thought he was looking for: "Let's drink it." So between five of us we drank the lot less a few tots we gave to the mess next door. It was a good job we were not required to do anything that afternoon.

That incident apart, I did well on rum. I think that, to some extent, I was pitied, as I would shortly be returning to civilian life. I was often given at least 'gulpers' out of a tot and one able seaman who was the navigator's yeoman said I could have his tot most days as he only wanted it on days that he felt cold. In any case he was working closely with officers, often doing delicate work such as correcting charts and did not wish to make a fool of himself. But I tried not to over do it and had the following story as a warning.

Our mess included Nick, a young able seaman, who was very much in love. Every evening, whether in port or at sea, he wrote at least a page to his fiancée. He never went ashore and although officially entitled to his tot, he rarely drank it. Then one day it was Nick's twenty-first birthday. There was no sign of him at tot-time, which was just as well since Shiner was inviting all us rum drinkers to make a contribution to one or more tots as a birthday present for Nick. He was a member of the gunner's party and Shiner explained that the petty officer of that squad had taken Nick along to the petty officer's mess where he intended to give Nick his own tot.

Apparently it did not end there as we found out later that others in the PO's mess had also treated him. By the time Nick appeared in our mess he had really acquired a taste for 'bubbly' and downed our donations with hardly a pause. Then the mess next door invited him to a similar ceremony. Shortly after that we were summoned back to work and heard no more until we returned to the mess at around four o'clock.

We were sitting around drinking the tea and eating the snacks provided by Shiner when the leading hand of the mess asked whether anyone had seen Nick lately. Shiner reported that he had visited the mess around 3pm to be violently sick in the mess-kid normally used for fag ends and other rubbish. Shiner had cleared it up but had been so engrossed in the task he had not noticed Nick's departure.

"We'd better have a look for him," said the leading hand, with an ominous glance to the back of the mess where there was a door leading to an open space only separated from the sea by guard-rails. Between us we had, by now, a pretty good knowledge of the ship's layout, but a search revealed no trace of Nick.

"I reckon he's gone over the side," said the leading hand gloomily. "I'll have to report this to the officer of the watch soon. Then we'll be for it for getting him drunk."

Just then the petty officer of the gunner's party put his head inside the mess.

"I've found Nick," he announced to our immense relief. "'E's a-kip in one of the gun turrets." Of course, we hadn't thought of that. Nick, as a member of the gunner's party would have access to the keys of the various gun emplacements. He'd obviously let himself into one to sleep it off. Later that evening he crept back onto the mess deck and thereafter went back to sobriety and letters to the fiancée.

Our trials took us to Scotland, where the weather was vile at that time of the year. But it didn't seem so, working several decks down in a huge ship under perpetual artificial light, usually in just shirt and trousers. One day, I was standing in for one of the others whose round took him into the island structure of the carrier. Seeing a door marked 'flight deck'. I decided to get some fresh air, opened it and stepped out into a raging blizzard. Unfortunately the door had pulled to behind me and it took me some time to reopen it and I staggered back into the island covered in snow. That cured curiosity about fresh air.

Somewhere off Rothesay a drifter carrying supplies, mainly potatoes, met us. Once these were loaded, it was announced that the drifter would take a limited number of non-duty men ashore. Most of us didn't fancy it, what with the snow and the cold, but two from my mess did go, one a newly promoted leading seaman, the other a quiet, regular ordinary seaman.

When they were settled in a pub ashore, the ordinary seaman confided that he had had enough of the Navy and wished to go home. A bit later, he went to the toilet and did not return. The leading seaman, very conscious of how easily he could lose his new rate, searched for him and very soon spied him trudging through snow-filled fields at the back of the pub. He set off in pursuit and quickly caught up with the lad. Somehow, possibly by the use of physical violence, he got him back to the pub and then explained the error of his ways. They both returned to the ship, but the leading hand said that he had not enjoyed his 'run' ashore.

A big carrier like Victorious carried a crew of nearly 2,000 when fully manned and, naturally some of them were bad characters. In DCHQ we were blessed with two, one a stoker and the other a naval airman. The stoker appeared to have a death wish of some sort and just could not avoid trouble. He had a feud running with a stoker PO, who was one of the watchkeepers in DCHQ and, despite the petty officer being ridiculously lenient with him, eventually went too far and was dismissed from the ship to serve a spell in a Naval prison. We heard that somehow he managed to escape from detention and was eventually picked up as a deserter and dismissed from the service. This was probably what he wanted all along.

The naval airman had recently been discharged from prison, having, allegedly, served a sentence for thieving from his messmates. This was considered by the lower deck to be the worst of all crimes and he was treated with deep suspicion and shunned, as far as possible. But he seemed pleasant enough to me and I couldn't help wondering whether there had been some miscarriage of justice.

The, one day, the main hot water pipe to the galley burst. The cooks promptly bailed out leaving hot water pouring down the corridor that led to the galley. All available hands in DCHQ, ventilation party included, were despatched to the galley area to deal with the situation. Our petty officer took charge and found that it was possible to access the corridor from a petty officers' mess that had a door that opened on to it. We gathered in the doorway and discussed what to do. The PO proposed that, if the water was deep enough, we make a raft out of bathroom gratings and float our lightest man down to where he could operate a stopcock to turn the water off. But it was pointed out that the 'current' would be against the raft. Naturally no one fancied wading through near boiling water. Suddenly the flow stopped. While we had been debating, our suspect naval airman had done a 'human fly' act along one of the bulkheads, using what hand holds he could, and reached the stopcock. After that he became something of a hero and the antipathy towards him ceased.

The food onboard Victorious was excellent. I was, however, somewhat alarmed when I first ate in the mess hall, which was right up forrard under the flight deck. I was presented with a metal tray, hollowed out into a number of compartments. One of these, I gathered, took the main course, another the sweet and a third the starter, if any. Not going to get much into this, was my first reaction. But I was wrong, the compartments were much deeper than I thought and held quite a quantity. The meals provided were breakfast (cereal and a cooked course), dinner (generally something substantial, like roast beef with all the trimmings, followed by spotted dick), high tea (a fry up) and a supper (a cake or other snack, served in our messdeck). I can only remember one failure and that was a supper. Posters appeared advertising that night's supper – Victorious oggies (Cornish pasties). Oggies being a favourite dish of the lower deck, these were awaited eagerly. When they arrived, however, they were frightful, containing only very tough meat and no onions, carrots, potato, etc. Not recommended.

The NAAFI supplied other amenities. In addition to the main shop, there was a cigarette bar and a goffa bar. A goffa was a fruit drink, very popular at that time, that gave rise to the expression "Go me, I'm a goffa." The cigarette bar sold everything related to smoking activities and the duty free prices were so cheap that Passing Cloud, Black Russian and other normally exotic brands were the most smoked. The main shop sold everything from chocolate bars to shampoo. There were other useful facilities on board, for example, in the evening, the laundry staff would come round undercutting their own prices – "Dhoby your overalls for threepence." I am sure the profits made found a good home not related to the normal laundry fund.

During this time I had been engaged in passing for able seaman. This involved written and practical exams and steering the ship for twelve hours. In my spare time I took myself off to the lower steering position to practice this art. This small compartment was situated deep in the bowels of the ship and was reached by vertical ladders. It was an interesting climb down for I discovered compartments that I never knew existed, such as the sail loft, where two sail makers, both chiefs, worked. Sail makers on an aircraft carrier? Well, as they explained, they had plenty to do for they repaired all canvas on board from dinghy sails and boat covers to the giant awnings sometimes erected on the flight deck for 'functions'.

In the steering position three men were on duty – a quartermaster and two telegraphists. Normally one of them would steer the ship while the other two got on with the important things of life – reading papers and paperbacks and doing crosswords or even their washing. They were delighted to see me, for while I did the steering all three could relax. Ten minutes instruction, mainly on the use of the gyro repeater, and I took over. It was an easy job, there was no weight on the wheel and, at sea, there were few changes of course. I clocked up my twelve hours in a few sessions and then took the rest of the exam.

The practical side was mainly knots and splices and the written side subjects such as the rule of the road at sea and anchors and cables. Chief examiner on the practical side was the ship's chief boatswain's mate who later told me that my back splice was such a mess that he should have failed me on that alone, but since I had scored 100 per cent on the written paper, he couldn't. So there I was a fully-fledged AB on about another threepence a day.

For Victorious' final trial the captain was evidently ordered to steam out into the Atlantic and find a gale to test her seaworthiness. We set out on this mission but first we had another drama. I have mentioned that newspapers and mail were brought on board by helicopter and this was a daily event if conditions permitted. On this particular day, the sea began to get up while the chopper was ashore. Expecting an exciting landing a large crowd gathered on the flight deck. The helicopter came in cautiously but just as it touched down, a big sea brought the ship up to meet it. The tail rotor dug into the deck and bits of it were flung into the crowd. Three men were injured, one so badly that he later died. That was the end of audiences for helicopter landings.

Then we certainly met our gale. Flight and cable decks were out of bounds with all doors leading to them sealed off. Immediately aft of the cable deck was the supply messdeck where water poured out of the ventilation system. Despite repeated calls to look at the problem there was nothing either the ventilation party or DCHQ could do about it. Then the ship suddenly slowed down. "Can't take it," said the wiseacres. And then the captain came on the ship's broadcast and explained that we had broken something called an A-bracket, which held one of the propellers on. We limped back to Portsmouth. There the captain cleared lower deck and announced that we would be going into dry dock to have the trouble put right. After that we would pay a courtesy visit to France, fly on the squadrons and then sail for a tour of

America. By my reckoning, I was due for demob about the time of the French visit. The skipper went on to say that, in the circumstances, he would be generous with leave – we could have two long weekends and one short one off per month for the three months that we would be in the dry dock. So there I was back home most weekends. Some people didn't believe that I was in the Navy.

While we were in the dry dock I ran foul of my old enemy – the lieutenant who had ordered me to run the errand out of Chatham Barracks and was now on the staff of Victorious. It was customary for ratings returning from weekend leave to catch the last possible train from Waterloo to Portsmouth, arriving at about three in the morning. For some reason, this time, several of us did not go to Aggie Weston's and went straight back to the ship. There the lieutenant did the unthinkable and lined us up on the quarterdeck for inspection. Since most of us had been asleep on the train our uniforms were not exactly perfect and he found fault with each and every one of us. We were told to report to him at seven a.m. with the offending items corrected. This meant further loss of precious sleep and was not popular. I, however, was told to report with a clean lanyard and merely borrowed one.

Shortly after this the officer received his come-uppance. A captain's inspection was announced and everything had to be gleaming, gleaming, gleaming! The officer visited a bathroom where a Chief PO was in charge of cleaning.

"Chief," the officer said, "the lagging round that steam pipe is disgusting. Take it down."

"I can't do that, sir. Steam pipes have to be protected."

"Take it down. That's an order." So down came the lagging.

When the captain came round he didn't notice the missing lagging. But in his retinue was the commander (engineering) who did and went bananas, since lagging came under his department. The over-zealous lieutenant received an official reprimand.

For a time, I was loaned from the ventilation party to help with a new concept called routine maintenance. For this I was placed with two chief shipwrights, largely to carry their tools. The theory was that we would work our way round the ship, checking that every valve, stopcock and other similar devices actually worked, greasing them or taking other remedial action where necessary. The area chosen for this trial was the hangar deck and according to the diagrams supplied to us there were literally hundreds of things to look at. The two chiefs took an executive decision and thereafter we only looked at one item in six, thereby leaving ample time for the important things in life, tea, crosswords, etc.

Shortly after that, I had a job change permanently, for it was the policy of the seaman division to change everybody's job every three months. My new job was working 'part of ship', in other words all the painting and cleaning jobs in my part of ship, the foc'sle. Victorious was out of dry dock by then and the decision had been taken that she must look smart for the French visit and therefore all available hands should 'paint ship'.

An aircraft carrier was too big for the conventional staging to be used so surrounding the ship in netting solved the problem. This came in sheets about ten feet square, which were tied together with spun yarn or similar, until a whole chunk of the ship was encased. We sailors would then climb into the netting with our paint pots and brushes and slap 'crab fat', or Admiralty grey paint as it was officially known, around to our hearts' content. All went well until the carrier Albion, which was leaving the dry dock just ahead of us, was carried into us by the wind. Several dozen sailors vacated the nets rather rapidly, but no harm was done to either ship.

Eventually we of the foc'sle division finished coating the forrard part of the ship and the nets had to be removed. The petty officer who was captain of the foc'sle addressed us: "I want two volunteers who can swim – Leading Seaman Ford and Able Seaman Dent."

"I'm not a good swimmer, P.O." I protested.

"Can you make from here to the jetty?" I told him that I could, just about.

"That's good enough. Now the pair of you get over the side and cut the nets adrift. The rest of us will pull them inboard."

There followed one of the most nerve-wracking hours of my life. Armed with sharp knives, Ford and I worked our way round the nets assessing which one should be cut adrift next. At the front of our minds was our own safety for we had no wish to deposit ourselves in the water. Inevitably we had several near misses but managed to complete the task without a ducking.

The ship was now within a few days of sailing for France and still no sign of my transfer to Chatham for demobilisation. Was I again the victim of an administrative cock-up? I didn't wish to have to travel back from France, far less to be carried off to America when I could be a civilian again. To make sure of my fate I submitted a request to be transferred to shore, which my officer gave a fair hearing. Then things happened quickly and, almost before I knew it, I was back in Chatham.

RETURN TO THE PLA

There was hardly anyone I knew from Barrack Guard days left at Chatham. For my last few days I worked 'part of ship'. But it was a hectic last few days. First I was summoned to the pay office where a pretty Wren officer informed me that my RNVR pay, which had ceased when I retrained as a seaman, was to be reinstated and back-dated. Although only sixpence per day, it amounted to quite a sum and went into my fund for a boat of my own.

Then I was piped to report to the seamen's regulating office where a motley group of sailors had assembled and I wondered what we had in common. A chief soon enlightened me. "Tomorrow," he announced, "we have a sports day against the Army at the Rugby Ground. All you men have athletics on your records as one of your hobbies, so you are our team. I have decided which events each of you will compete in."

He read from a list. When he reached the bit: "Able Seaman Dent you will do the one hundred and two-twenty yards," I felt that I had to protest. I had been a cross-country runner at school not a sprinter and had only given athletics as a sport for my record as I felt that I ought to have something besides sailing. But his mind was made up and he obviously did not wish to waste any more of his valuable time on the project. So I competed in the two sprint races and, much to my surprise, did not come last, but certainly not first. Overall, the Navy did badly.

I was duty watch on my last night in the Navy. The last job I wanted on this final night was that of outside escort which entailed travelling anywhere in the country to pick up any deserters apprehended by the police. It could mean a delay in being discharged if the escort was required to go any distance. Sure enough, I drew this as my duty and there was a prisoner to pick up in Leeds. I mentioned my bad luck on the mess deck. And a voice shouted out: "Did you say Leeds? I live there!" The owner of the voice bustled over and suggested an exchange of duties since he thought that he would get a chance to see his wife and family while formalities regarding the prisoner were completed. His duty was fire picket, a sinecure unless there was a fire, so I was pleased and relieved to swap. There was no fire.

Just prior to this I met an 'old friend'. At least, that was what he insisted that he was, although I did not remember him. He certainly knew a lot about me, even addressing me as 'Dicky' which was my nickname in the Barrack Guard (I was known as 'George' on Victorious). He claimed to have known me in training and afterwards in Chatham. He said he was to be released on the same day as I and suggested that we do our demob routine together and then share the traditional taxi to the station. But first, he said, we must celebrate our release by going out on the town on our last non-duty night.

So we had a night out that was a bit low key with just the two of us. We had a meal in Chatham NAAFI club, followed by a few beers and a half-hearted attempt to pick up girls from the NAAFI dance hall. When I came to do the demob routine, visiting the doctor, dentist, etc. and handing back items of kit, there was no sign of my friend so I went round without him. And there he was standing outside the last place that I had to visit, dressed in his working uniform.

"Why aren't you doing the routine?" I asked him.

"Well," he said, "it's like this. The judge gave me the choice of staying in the Navy or prison. So I'm staying in."

"But what was that all about the other night? Celebrating our release?"

"I just thought you ought to have a good time before you left." A true but mysterious friend, indeed.

Shortly after that I had my taxi to the station, sharing with some others that I had met during the demob routine. And that was the end of my career in the Royal Navy, such as it was. Readers will have noticed the frequent references to crosswords, cups of tea, chief petty officers with little to do, etc. It has to be remembered that the prime purpose of a warship is to fight battles and she must carry sufficient men to man her weapons in a conflict. This is far in excess of those needed for peacetime operation. Similarly shore establishments have to be able to supply a reserve of personnel and provide the necessary back up. The spare men have to be found something to do, however minor. Hence the ventilation party, routine maintenance, etc.

At least one pundit has stated that life in the Navy (and indeed all armed forces) is ninety per cent boredom and, after my experiences, I wouldn't disagree with this theory. It is amply demonstrated by

A dockland scene. Sailing barge 'Royalty' in the Royal Docks

Author's collection

something that happened to me during my early days in the Navy.

I had been given a broom and told to sweep a passageway. After ten minutes I had completed the task to my satisfaction and reported so to the leading seaman in charge.

"Sweep it again, then," was his response. When I reported for the third time he said in exasperation: "Look, that is your job for this morning. There's nothing else. Now use your soddin' loaf an' look busy at it or lose yourself somewhere."

And they also say you only remember the good bits and I am probably as guilty of this as anyone else.

So I spent a month's demobilisation leave on sailing and other related activities, missing the daily tot of rum badly. Then it was time to go back to work. When I was called up, I had no intention of returning to the Port of London but now it was a case of the 'devil you know' and, in due course, I reported to head office for re-employment. I attended the establishment (or staff) department where I was ushered in to the presence of what I assumed to be a very high official. Imperiously he informed me that my old job awaited me (No! Not wharfage and porterage and filing!). Such was his manner that I forgot that I intended to ask for a transfer to Tilbury Docks and I meekly accepted India and Millwall Docks again.

Some years later, by then at the Royal Docks, I worked with my interviewer and, far from being a high official, he was the same grade as myself. He was half-Swedish and was so proficient at that language that he did Swedish translations as a sideline. I need not have worried about asking for a transfer.

So once again I was interviewed by Mr. Tooth. His attitude, this time, was much friendlier and he even seemed glad to get me back. No talk of smuggling or theft this time. He informed me that I could go back on to export charges but, if I was interested, there was a vacancy on tonnage dues. If I wanted it, all I had to do was ask the new principal clerk who had replaced Jeffries.

This gentleman readily agreed to my joining tonnage dues. He was a very different type to Jeffries, addressing the staff by their Christian names and only expecting them to call him "Mister" and not "Sir". His attitude to overtime was the opposite of Jeffries, for it seemed almost continuous, both in the evenings and on Sundays. Admittedly there was probably more work around, but there seemed to be an open house with people attending the general office from all over the dock to do overtime. And it did not end there. I thought that I would go in one Sunday. I arrived a bit early and found myself surrounded by strangers. I asked who they were and was told that they had come up from the Royal Docks where there was currently no overtime.

There had been other changes while I had been away. George was gone back to his beloved Surrey Docks and Jack had also just departed. Because of his attendance problems he had been continually moved around the general office, ending up in tonnage dues. Now he was being given a fresh start at London docks and I was, in fact, his replacement. It was soon established that I was a pipe-smoker and I was offered a drawer full of pipes that Jack had left behind. These were all of the curly stemmed Meerschaum variety and had all been lovingly smoked, as borne out by the dried spittle around the mouthpieces. I declined them, with thanks.

But George and Jack were more than adequately replaced by a new character – Mr. Hopkins or Hoppy, another refugee from Surrey Docks, but without George's bitterness. Always turned out in a dark suit, bowler hat and regimental tie, he would arrive for work in bicycle clips, as he cycled from somewhere south of the river. Hoppy disliked officialdom and gave an early demonstration of this. We were expecting a visit from someone high up in the PLA – a board member or somebody like that. Attempts were made to tidy the office up before his arrival. Eventually Hoppy could stand it no longer and, springing on to a desk, cried: "Whatever you do, when the big-wig gets here, he'll take one look and say "Pigsty!" And who lives in a pigsty? Pigs!" He, too, was transferred to tonnage dues and became an endless source of amusement.

Later when we were working at South West India, Hoppy arrived one morning on his bicycle in thick fog. A lorry driver pulled up and asked him for directions to N shed, South West India Dock.

"Straight ahead and over the bridge," Hoppy replied, "you can't miss it."

Then with a great cry of "Oh! My God!" he remounted his machine and tore after the disappearing lorry.

"What was all that about?" I asked when he returned.

"I told him straight ahead and if he'd done that he have driven straight over the edge into the cutting in the fog. I didn't tell him to veer right." But of course the lorry driver had realised and gone over the bridge.

Basically tonnage dues, or the dues, office rendered charges incurred by ships and barges using the India and Millwall Docks system. These included, as well as the actual dues, charges for towage and for the costs of loading and/or discharging. For the latter two systems were in operation, for the PLA did their own discharging in West India Dock and charged the shipping company for the whole process but in Millwall Docks private firms of stevedores were used, but there were certain recoverable costs for the PLA, such as the hire of quay cranes. overtime and a charge for labour standing by in certain circumstances.

The dues office also appeared to be a dumping ground for those charges that didn't seem to belong to any other office. These included the supply of water and electricity, the hire of floating cranes, royalties on compressors, etc. working on the quays, the hire of PLA police to escort a heavy load or a payroll and charges for the use of outside ambulances to take members of ships' crews to hospital. There were probably several others but these will do as an example. My first job was largely dealing with these miscellaneous charges.

Some of them occurred infrequently and to help with this, and other problems that arose within the office, we kept a large book of 'case histories' – mainly memos from head office solving past problems. Some wag had stuck a piece of paper to the outside of this volume quoting the chapter and verse of a Shakespearean quotation – when researched it came out as "bloody instructions which returneth to avenge themselves upon the inventor."

The Fifties and Sixties were a boom time for the India and Millwall Docks. At times we were flooded out with ships, even having the odd one moored to buoys in the middle of the dock to discharge overside to lighters while the Canary Wharf berth often had two alongside with one laying 'second bottom' to the other. Among the well-known lines using the dock were Ellerman Lines, Furness-Withy, Ben Line, T & J Harrison and United States Lines. Millwall Docks contained the Central Granary where complete cargoes of grain were often discharged and also specialised in timber and paper products from the Baltic and

Scandinavia. Strick Line vessels also loaded there for the Middle East.

Millwall Docks were enlivened by the fortnightly visits of two cargo-passenger liners, Suecia and Britannia. These two elegant ships, both built in 1929, ran between London and Gothenburg. Their passengers were dropped at Tilbury landing stage and they came on to Millwall to discharge their cargo, whichever one was due arriving at lunchtime on Monday. They moored at B & C Sheds, Millwall and were held off from the quay by a pontoon or dummy so that craft could be loaded between the ship and the quay.

But the great thing about these two ships was that they carried stewardesses of the blonde, Scandinavian goddess type. Stories about these girls were legion and here are two of the more repeatable ones.

A crane driver was lifting cargo out of the Suecia and, seated high in his crane's cabin, he could look down on the entire ship. Suddenly he spotted a stewardess on the ship's boatdeck wearing, so far as he could see, only a towel. She took some time to select a spot in the sun and then took the towel off to sunbathe. She was, indeed, wearing nothing underneath. The crane driver was so busy watching that he forgot the load that he had just lifted out of the Suecia and 'splat!' against the side of the warehouse went a large case of Swedish glassware. An interesting insurance claim followed.

Next to B & C sheds was, of course, A shed that handled small cargo-only ships from Scandinavia. One night A shed's supervisor was in his office catching up on paperwork while outside a small ship was being discharged. The supervisor suddenly realised that it had gone very quiet on the quay. Suspecting a lightning strike by dockworkers he went out to investigate. There was not a soul around, cargo was hanging from quay cranes, vehicles were abandoned, and mugs of tea left half finished.

But down the quay at B & C sheds a large crowd of men was on the pontoon holding Britannia off the quay. The supervisor walked down there to see what was going on. As he drew near he realised that the mob included dockers, lightermen, tally clerks, foremen and even customs officers. They were pushing and shoving one another and he could hear cries of "It's my turn next" and "You pushed in." Spotting his foreman at the back of the crowd, he enquired what was going on. The foreman explained that there was a cabin on a level with the pontoon. Inside it was a stewardess performing a striptease for half a crown per item.

Each day the dues office would receive a bag from the dockmaster's department. In it would be the dockmaster's reports that listed all shipping movements for the previous day or days if a weekend intervened. There would also be ships' declarations for those ships that had entered the dock during that period together with towage orders when tugs were employed. Also included were documents relating to the movement of lighters – a docking note for those that had entered the dock and passes for those that had left together with a craft report that summarised all the movements. More on the arrangements for lighters later on.

The ship's declaration was the official evidence that the ship had entered the docks and gave her details – name, agent, where from, tonnage, etc. It was supposed to be signed by the captain but that didn't always happen. One day Hoppy decided to have a purge on unsigned declarations and despatched me to a Yugoslav ship to obtain the missing signature. I wandered around the ship's accommodation, not seeing a soul, until I found a galley where a cook was working. Largely

'Sun XXI', a ship-towing tug

S. Emery collection

113

A typical dock scene – a ship, a barge and some lighters
Author's collection

by sign language, I indicated to him that I required the captain's signature on the document. He went off and shortly returned with two officers who, by their insignia, I gathered to be the second mate and third engineer. The latter could speak a form of English and managed to convey that the captain was not aboard and could the second mate sign as the senior officer present?

Of course he could because I was getting fed-up with the whole business and Hoppy wouldn't know any different. So that was that problem solved.

A few days later, we had another unsigned declaration, this time from a Dutch coaster that had gone through West India Dock to Poplar Dock, the small British Railways dock that could only be reached via the main dock complex. Hoppy decided to deal with it himself. Once he had explained the problem to the captain, out came the schnapps bottle.

"Ah! Meester PLA! I am so sorry, I do not sign. You stay for leedle drink?"

Several schnapps and one signature later, Hoppy returned looking very pleased with himself. If only, I thought, I had drawn the Dutch ship.

Towage orders indicated the number of tugs used to dock a ship and who owned them. Towage arrangements were somewhat complicated. Basically ship towage on the river was performed by private enterprise in the shape of several towage companies – W. H. J. Alexander, Ship Towage and Gaselee. Towage in the docks was by the PLA, who maintained one and sometimes two tugs in the dock for this purpose. This often meant a change of tugs at the lock into the dock. Once the ship was in the lock the private tugs would slide out and when the water in the lock reached dock level and the inner gates were open the PLA tugs would slide in to take over. Much later on, when I was at Royal Docks, a PLA tug, when performing this manoeuvre, was caught by the ship's propeller, which sliced her side open. The tug master managed to get her into the basin clear of the lock where she quickly sank. The crew rowed ashore in the tug's boat, bearing their prize possession – an early colour television set.

But very often PLA tugs could not cope with all the shipping movements in the dock; for example some of the bigger ships needed three tugs, especially in a high wind. Then the 'outside' tugs were allowed in to help out. Hence the need to know who had performed the towage for charges had to be sorted out with the towage companies. Sometimes, to settle a claim for damages, a towage order had to be forwarded to the claims department at head office. Like all communications with head office, this was done via the dock superintendent's office. Eventually the towage orders would return, accompanied by a slip that stated 'detach your document and file' and signed by the superintendent's chief clerk, a gentleman affectionately known to one and all as "The Mongolian fuck pig". One day he phoned me up and accused me of not handling the towage orders properly. In vain, I protested that I had been doing exactly what his slips said, detaching the documents and filing them. Oh no, he retorted, I should write on the back of the slip 'document detached and filed' and sign it over my office stamp. There was no clue anywhere that this was what should be done. Such are the ways of officialdom.

Sailing barges, or sailormen, as they were known in the docks, were rather a twilight area. There was, first of all, some uncertainty as to whether they should be treated as ships and given a declaration or as lighters and given the docking note that applied to lighters. This was further complicated by the fact that only outside the port limits, defined by a line from Walton-on-the-Naze to the North Foreland, were they required to pay dues as vessels trading coastwise. The dues paid by coasting vessels were entered in a ledger designated No. 7 and from this volume it was possible to extract sailing barge movements.

In the dues book room, I unearthed an old No.7 ledger dating from the 1930s and, of course, back then not only were sailing barge movements much more numerous but they were by genuine sailing barges, generally without powered assistance. All sailings between West India Docks and ports outside PLA limits – Ipswich, Yarmouth, Mistley, Dover, and so on – were covered. Realising that this ledger would be an invaluable artefact to those interested in sailing barge history, I enquired whether I could acquire it, with money if necessary, either for myself or for the fledgling barge research organisation that I knew had stared recently. The answer was that it would not be possible, as some of the barge owners mentioned were still in business and might not like their business, however ancient, made public. A recent visit to the archives of the Museum in Docklands, which is doing a splendid job in preserving what remains of dockland life, has established that neither this ledger nor any similar document has survived. They were probably all burnt as PLA offices were demolished when the docks closed.

Sailing barges had a fairly hard time in the docks. They were not liked by the dockers, who preferred to load the modern steel lighters that were much easier to stow cargo in. "Fuckin' sailormen. Burn the fuckin' lot, I say," was a frequent docker comment. There was little love lost between sailing barge crews and lightermen either. The big steel lighters, if badly handled, could do a lot of damage to a barge's rails and boat davits. For this reason sailormen established a number of quiet mooring places or lay-bys within the docks where they hoped to lie unmolested.

The crew of one sailorman, trading frequently to the Surrey Docks, took a dislike to a certain lighterman who always seemed to make a target of their barge. They bided their time until they became aware of the lighterman directing his craft towards them on a dark night. As he approached they shrouded themselves in the barge's white jibs and then, as he was about to moor up to the barge, they rose up, still shrouded in white and clanking the anchor chain which was stowed on deck. The lighterman moved his craft away in a hurry and troubled them no more.

Another complication for the barges that it was clearly stated on the back of docking notes that sailing was forbidden within the docks. Towage would have been expensive so most barges still sailed albeit under very reduced canvas, secure in the knowledge that the practice was 'winked at'. As engines became more common in barges, towage could often be performed by a powered vessel of the same owners as the sailorman at no cost.

I must admit that, at this stage, my interest in the sailing barge was waning. Plenty of them were still about in the docks, but most were now motorised and it was rare to see one that was a pure sailing vessel. Virtually every week, I would see one of the former auxiliary barges cut down to power only. It was all rather sad and for this reason, I kept no records. This is now regretted, since, working in the dues office, I had ample opportunity to record movements and even those of motor barges would now be of historic interest.

However there were still some sailormen around and a grain ship at the Central Granary, Millwall would attract a handful. It was there that I saw West's big auxiliary Leonard Piper on what was probably her last voyage before her owners went out of business and Francis & Gilders' Alaric, by then renamed Balarice when her original name was required for an ocean-going ship. Elsewhere I sighted Everard's Lady Maud and their racing barge Sara looking very ordinary on a routine cargo-carrying voyage.

I had not been in tonnage dues very long when it was decided to relocate the office to South West India Dock, for reasons that were never specified. The move was achieved by piling all the furniture into a trailer that was hauled through the dock by a tractor with myself and Hoppy, complete with bowler hat, perched on top of the pile of furniture.

Our relocation made a considerable difference to travelling arrangements. Now I had, in addition to the walk from Stepney East

Station to the dock gates, an additional hike through the docks. All very well on a bright summer's day and there was plenty to look at, but it wasn't so funny in rain and wind. Moreover there was no direct bus service although it was possible to pick up a No. 56 at the top of West India Dock Road, go to Byng Street and enter the dock through a side entrance that was near the office. Many of my colleagues used to hitch lifts on the backs of lorries but I was loath to do this as a docker was killed outside my former office when the lorry he had just jumped off inadvertently reversed over him.

Walking through the dock was made interesting by the PLA railway system. Still steam powered at this time, there seemed no limit to the number of goods wagons that one of the tiny engines would endeavour to pull. Since the lines crossed and then ran along the roadways, all other traffic, whether vehicular or pedestrian, had to wait while a train crept past. For a fortnight I was fortunate to borrow a racing bike from a colleague while he was on leave. The bike was kept at Stepney East Station and from there I had to negotiate the terrifying traffic on Commercial Road before the somewhat quieter West India Dock Road. Once inside the dock on my first ride, I found the bike uncontrollable. It seemed to have a mind of its own and to be taking me off to some destination of its own choosing. Then I realised that its wheels were locked into the railway lines. All things considered, I found it easier to leave by the Byng Street gate and take the back streets to the station when on the bike.

But the PLA railway system did have its uses. My section leader, head of the dues office, was in the habit of staying a bit late to clear up outstanding work. One night he was walking through the dock in pouring rain when he heard a railway engine snorting along behind him. As it drew level it stopped and a voice shouted: "Jump aboard, mate!" He became the only man I know to have had a lift on the footplate of a PLA railway engine!

After a while we had a new section leader, transferred from the grain ledgers where he had spent most of his working life. Benny claimed that he had been transferred against his will, professed not to be interested in tonnage dues and spent most of days dozing and just signing documents placed in front of him, until he was sent back to the familiar placid waters of grain ledgers. But Benny and his son were keen racing motorcyclists and Benny rode one to work, which was surprising since his eyesight was terrible. One Saturday morning he asked me when my next train was. I replied that it was a four minutes past twelve but I did not expect to catch it as I had a twenty-minute walk after leaving the office at twelve.

"I'll get you there," said Benny.

There ensued the most terrifying pillion ride of my life with Benny weaving in and out of huge lorries on Commercial Road at 70mph. I caught the train all right, but was halfway down the line before I stopped shaking.

The office building at South West India Dock contained, in addition to tonnage dues, the operational and ledger offices and canteen for all the staff of South West India Dock. We reported to the principal clerk of the ledger office, another of the PLA's characters. A copious pipe smoker, he would spend hours at a time in his cubbyhole of an office staring at the far wall and puffing clouds of blue smoke. At the end of one of these sessions he would spring into action and come out with a solution, often outrageous, to one of the office's problems. He was known to dabble in the occult and his self styled 'secretary' claimed that during the pipe smoking sessions he was consulting a Tibetan monk who was his adviser on office matters.

This principal clerk, Joe, pretended to be a strict disciplinarian and insisted on explanations for lateness in the mornings. At the time my railway line, the London, Tilbury and Southend was converting from steam to electric power. Delays were numerous and unpredictable in both frequency and length. I was often quite a bit late in the mornings. Joe said that he fully understood and if I put train delay as my excuse in the attendance book as my excuse then he would initial it and I would hear no more.

This was good as the rule was that if you were late more than three times in one month, then you had to explain yourself to the docks superintendent in what tended to be a painful interview. If, however, my principal clerk had authorised my lateness due to unavoidable circumstances then, I considered, there would be no interview. But there was and, although Mr. Tooth was sympathetic, he still felt that I could cure the problem by catching an earlier train. I explained that, since the trains could be anything up to two hours late, this was unlikely to be the solution. In the end, he advised me to do what I could to improve matters. Later, Joe said that he could only authorise lateness when the delay was mentioned in the newspapers, but I suspected that the Tibetan monk had taken a hand. Fortunately for me the work on the railway work had passed its crucial stage and I wasn't late so much after that.

After a few months the dues office was on the move again, but only to the upper floor of the building. This had a number of advantages. We were remote from the eagle eye of Joe and were largely left to get on with things. Moreover we were across the corridor from the canteen. This was run by a 22-stone cook called Lil, assisted by Kath, who was not quite so large but one of the ugliest women I had ever seen. Nevertheless she had a heart of gold and became an embarrassment to me. Kath controlled the puddings and must have felt that I needed 'building up'. Every time I asked her for a pudding, she would wink and slide a second portion on to my plate. Since the puddings tended to be of the stodgy, jam roly-poly variety, my weight began to leap up. In desperation, I took the option of having a cheese roll, which was always available. Kath soon cottoned on and I would be handed a plate containing two. I tried not having a sweet at all, but this worried Kath and she constantly enquired after my health. Eventually I persuaded her that one portion would do, but she obviously did not like it.

Generally the food at South West India was very good, but subject to fluctuations. It was an operational department and the number of ships on the berths governed the amount of work. If the department was very busy extra staff would be drafted in from elsewhere to help out. These men would all take an early lunch and, for some reason the canteen would not be informed of their presence. Therefore there would be a run on the available food and those taking a late lunch would only be offered ham and chips, as Lil always seemed to have a reserve of these items. In the dues office we had teatime 'perk', as Lil would leave us a supply of bread and dripping at one penny a slice.

The ledger office, in true PLA form, had its characters. Among them was Ernie, a true glutton who, when curry was on the menu, would have the normal helping plus an extra jug of the mixture and a complete loaf. Ernie had worked his way up from messenger boy to second-in-command of the office and was apt to express himself in dockers' language unless he knew that someone of importance was present. Occasionally, tonnage dues would have a visitor from another port to see how we did things. Probably the most important of these was the chief accountant of the port of Piraeus in Greece. This gentleman, who could speak excellent English, was placed with one of the staff whose desk was just inside the door. After a while, the accountant offered one of his aromatic Greek cigarettes to his instructor. They had both just lit up when the door was flung open and there was Ernie, framed in the doorway.

"Christ!" he announced, "who's smokin' shit in here?" He spent the next ten minutes grovelling to the accountant.

LEIGH SAILING CLUB –
THE PLYWOOD YEARS

The late Fifties and early Sixties were years of considerable expansion for Leigh-on-Sea Sailing Club. The whole face of amateur sailing was changing, heavy wooden boats such as the TEOD and EOD, were declining in popularity as they were hard work and needed three people to sail them. Two-man dinghies built of plywood, such as the Yachting World General Purpose 14ft Dinghy (GP 14 for short) and the Enterprise were becoming increasingly popular. The snag was that such boats would not lie to a mooring and had to be kept ashore.

This was fine if your club had access to a field that could be turned into a dinghy park, as was the case at nearby Thorpe Bay Yacht Club, but Leigh Sailing Club had no such facility. However the club did have mooring rights for a vessel on the seafront. The borough council was persuaded that the space reserved for a club ship could be used for the site of a platform or 'rack' to store sailing dinghies complete with a slipway for launching them. The council's foreshore work force, normally employed on repairing groynes, did the heavier work, while club members did the lighter tasks, such as decking the platform.

The original structure was not very convenient, since boats had to be wheeled onto the public footpath to reach the slipway, disturbing the general public. So, within a few years, the rack was extended considerably outwards, giving two rows of boats with a central gangway to two slipways. Such was the expansion of dinghy sailing that the extra space was needed anyway.

Once the original rack was ready, those members with plywood boats moved on to it and were quickly followed by other new owners, myself included. The club's official dinghy class became the GP 14, which was sailed and raced by old and young alike. The GP 14s carried a symbol of a bell on their sails, which was said to represent the bells of Aberdovey. No doubt the Welsh resort was involved in the boat's origins. The Swift Catamaran Class provided a different type of sailing, small racing catamarans with two hulls, which provided some very fast sailing. The Swift's national association was based on the club, once it had been formed.

But it was the GP 14 Class that attracted me. I had been saving for a boat of my own since starting work and I was now able to buy the appropriately named Crosswinds from a Mr. Cross at Thorpe Bay. Cousin Simon and I sailed her round from Thorpe Bay to Leigh round the end of Southend Pier. A little work and she was fit for racing in the growing GP 14 Class at Leigh. Believing it to be bad luck to change a boat's name, I kept her as Crosswinds.

The expansion of the GP 14 Class within Leigh Sailing Club was rapid and it was not long before our average number of starters in club races was in double figures, with twenty-two recorded as competing in one race. And the class was not just involved in domestic racing: it was used for most of the team racing fixtures, including the Norwich Frostbite and some new events such as occasional races against the Port of London Authority Sailing Club. No prizes for guessing who arranged this match!

By then I was sailing secretary of Leigh Sailing Club. I had come into this job in a round about fashion, for I had been elected to the committee, at the tender age of twenty-one, as assistant secretary. The then-sailing secretary was one of life's characters. A retired Army major (cashiered for misappropriation of mess funds, we later found out), he did a splendid job of organising the club's sailing until the end of the sailing season in the autumn, then he disappeared. But he still had the annual prize giving to arrange. The committee worried that he might not carry out this important function but, on the night, there he was giving a really masterful performance with, as usual, a pint pot gripped firmly in one hand. However, after the event he told us that he would not be seeking re-election as he saw his future in the wider spectrum of yachting (which he later deprived of a considerable sum of money.)

So where was the club to find a new sailing secretary? I was somewhat bored with assistant secretary as it only concerned the supervision of the club's stock of badges, ties and other haberdashery, so I offered my services. The offer was accepted with alacrity and I was highly pleased. But, at the tender age of twenty-two, I was naïve and didn't realise that nobody really wanted these unpaid jobs and it was

G.P.14 'Crosswinds'

Author's collection

LSC slipway on a busy day

Author's collection

rare to have a volunteer.

The sailing secretary of a yacht or sailing club organises the club's official sailing. To this end he works out during the previous autumn the next season's programme. First of all, he has to pick suitable tides that do not necessitate competitors getting up at the crack of dawn or sailing in the dark. Anything that involves another club or organisation has to be agreed with them and it is normally found that they haven't even thought about the matter but will reach a decision, possibly, in a month's time. If the sailing secretary is lucky his programme is ready just as his club's literature goes to print in January.

The sailing secretary is also responsible for the sailing instructions, which are the rules that govern the club's racing. The Royal Yachting Association decides many of these, especially in more recent years, but there are always local conditions, particularly in tidal places, that have to be taken into account. Allied to this concept was the provision of buoys for the competitors to race round. At first, this was easy, for all the Southend yacht clubs subscribed to a fund to pay a local waterman to maintain the buoys and lay and retrieve them at the beginning and end of each sailing season. However, for various reasons, this admirable system was dropped and each club became responsible for its own buoys. This, of course, fell to the sailing secretaries and most promptly delegated it to their assistants. Generally the buoys were 40-gallon oil drums suitably painted and held in place by appropriate ground tackle. Their maintenance was not an easy job, as local fishermen, wildfowlers and just ordinary vandals seemed to make a target of racing marks which were variously run down, shot at and cast adrift.

At Leigh Sailing Club there were other complications. The sailing secretary was responsible for moorings and could spend many a happy hour traipsing over the mud at low tide to show boat owners a spare patch of mud where a mooring could be sunk and then explaining that only the site was provided and how the owner, often to his horror, would have to supply his own tackle and dig the necessary holes.

With the expansion of dinghy sailing, the sailing secretary, as a natural extension of the mooring job, became responsible for the maintenance and allocation of the dinghy racks, including, if the need arose, construction work. Admittedly plenty of help was at hand, but the job became onerous in the extreme and eventually anything to do with racks and moorings was farmed out, the racks becoming the responsibility of a new post on the committee.

But the highlight of the sailing secretary's year was the annual prize giving. Quite apart from the cups and trophies first, second and third in each race were given a cash prize – 10/-, 5/- and 2/6d respectively. But there was also an entry fee of 2/6d per race so those, and there were many, often including myself, who had entered, say, ten races and achieved a couple of third places, ended up owing the club money. Nevertheless, at the prize giving they would be called up for their two thirds, suitably applauded and would then retire to open their envelope to find it contained a bill.

But what an accounting headache for the poor sailing secretary! Everything had to balance and roughly equal the prize fund to which wealthier members had contributed during the year. Moreover he had to prepare a cash breakdown of so many coins of each denomination and inevitably he would end up by asking the bar for change.

But once the 'loot' had been distributed everyone relaxed. Those that had won cups circulated them once they had been filled with suitable

A mass start of G.P.14's

Author's collection

exotic and highly alcoholic mixtures. Those who had managed to beat the system and win sizeable amounts of money soon spent it on rounds of drinks for their crews and fellow competitors. While those who had earlier moaned at the size of their bills soon mellowed. The 'cash' prizes lasted for a surprisingly long time until it was realised that it was simpler to present the cups, etc., together with replicas and forget both entry fees and cash prizes.

But, I always thought, the main function of the sailing secretary was to encourage people to turn out for the races. In those days (the early Sixties) there was very little entertainment in the town other than the cinemas and the pubs and one could be pretty certain that the keener sailors would be in the club on Friday night, generally advertised as 'Club Night'. It was a comparatively easy exercise to wander round the clubhouse approaching individuals about future racing prospects. The approach had to vary, according to the known abilities and inclinations of each one – "You will be racing tomorrow, won't you?" "I expect you'll race tomorrow, as usual." "Have you ever considered racing?" – were three common gambits that speak for themselves. They generally worked.

In 1961, the club acquired its first rescue boat (or safety boat, as they should now be known). Named Jubilee to celebrate the club's first 50 years, she was a former Trinity House launch of the sort that was carried in davits by a much larger vessel and launched to take technicians over for a close look at a buoy. Trinity House tended to use these launches in all weathers and therefore she was a superb sea boat, if a little slow for the rescue task. She served the club for many years until pensioned off when a faster vessel was acquired. She went on to serve a local waterman and may still be afloat somewhere. The rescue boat was run by her own committee and did not come directly under the sailing secretary, but liaison was needed to ensure Jubilee's crews knew what was required of them.

Similar co-operation was needed with the race officers who actually started and finished the races. Inevitably the sailing secretary would be with these officials for the start of some races and, in any case, had to understand what was happening himself. Quite quickly he would become competent to stand in for a race officer himself and sometimes did so in an emergency.

So, if taken seriously, the post of sailing secretary was quite a complicated job. I ended up doing it for a total of eight years; eventually losing it for not taking rules too seriously, considering, using an old quote, "that rules were for the guidance of wise men and the adherence of fools," a view of mine that has yet to change.

Meanwhile there were plenty of adventures on the water, both at Leigh and elsewhere. One of these occurred during the inter-club team races when the yacht clubs of Southend-on-Sea and district reserve a day for team competitions for a number of ancient trophies. The races are all run at the same time with the clubs taking it in turn to act as host. This year it was the turn of Alexandra Yacht Club, whose clubhouse is right next to Southend Pier, with sailing courses that tend to be in the vicinity of the pier.

I was crewing on the gaff-rigged Boy Martin, mentioned earlier, in the Operatic Cup for handicapped dinghies while cousin Simon, on leave from the Navy, was crewing on a TEOD in a separate race. It was already quite windy and the boats in the various races had become quite mixed up when a gale-force squall struck. Fortunately Boy Martin had roller reefing and was already sailing with a reefed mainsail. Our helmsman saw the squall coming and we just had time to roll up the foresail. We were in close proximity to Southend Pier and had had several other boats near us, including Simon's TEOD, as the squall struck. In the bad visibility that accompanied the wind we could see none of them.

We gybed round, a dangerous manoeuvre in any fresh wind, let alone a near gale, and sailed back on our course, parallel to the Pier. A shout led us to the TEOD She had not only capsized but more or less sunk as well. The only bits visible were the top of her mast, with Simon clinging to it and the stern with the other two crew members hanging on to the main horse. One of them was a girl and she was obviously terrified and was hysterical.

In the severe conditions there was not much we could do other than stand by until further help arrived. That is until Simon lost his grip on the top of the mast and was rapidly being swept towards the pier. We started sailing again in a desperate attempt to rescue him, realising that we would probably only have one chance before he was too close to the pier. The owner sailed Boy Martin while us two crew members readied ourselves to snatch my cousin from the water. We just managed to grab him, largely by the hair, and swing him onboard. We then thought about picking up the other two, but by that time a speedboat had arrived from the pier and was pulling them out.

We all ended up on the pier head where we were treated as distressed mariners and issued with dry clothing and blankets. The lifeboat later towed Boy Martin home with the owner on board to steer her while the rest of us went home by road.

The TEOD was recovered at low water and was not too badly damaged.

Meanwhile, I had been racing Crosswinds with limited success. I had had a couple of third places and had once won a race when most of the fleet had sailed the wrong course. With such a large fleet sailing it became not so much the winning but the competition with boats of much the same performance. It was gratifying to say to a fellow competitor: " Beat you that time," when we had, in fact, finished ninth and tenth.

In the hopes of improving my performance, I ordered the first suit of Terylene sails for a GP 14 in Leigh Sailing Club. This was done under conditions of great secrecy, the newly arrived sails being tried out during the week when no-one was around. The first the fleet knew of my purchase was when I turned out for a race with the new sails. But my efforts were in vain, for, within a very short period, most of the others had acquired sails in the revolutionary new material.

One race in particular stands out. This was started in conditions that were already misty with a light easterly breeze. The course took us down to Westcliff, up to a buoy on the north bank of the Ray Channel and then back in to our starting line. By the time we reached the mark at Westcliff the mist had thickened into a proper fog. We rounded the mark and lost sight of the other competitors. I assured my crew that we stood every chance of winning this race since I knew the location of every fishing boat moored in the Ray. All we had to do was sail from one to another until we came to the one moored nearest to the mark close to the Ray. Then it would be a simple matter to sail in towards the shore and find the finishing line. In the circumstances the race officer would be bound to shorten the race to one round only and we would be certain winners.

At first this scheme worked well as first one fishing boat and then another loomed up through the murk until we were past the last one and could just make out the Ray mark. We rounded it and started sailing towards the shore but we had not gone far when we heard the sound of an engine behind us. Out of the fog came the club's newly acquired rescue boat Jubilee.

"Where do you think you are going?" they asked.

"Sailing in to the finishing line," I replied cockily.

"No you're not. You're headed towards Kent. You went round the buoy the wrong way. Follow us!"

We did as we were told and shortly afterwards passed the Ray mark for the second time.

"Reckon they were right," I said grudgingly.

Shortly after that we lost Jubilee, as the fog seemed even thicker. We sailed on and on without sighting anything at all bar the odd seagull. I became concerned, surely we should have sighted the shore by now? Had Jubilee's crew been correct or did we get it right first time? I decided to anchor and await developments. Once this was done we had a smoke and listened to see whether we could pick up any sound clues. We were reassured by one thing – by putting the anchor over we had established that we were not in very deep water!

After a while we both thought we heard a train so we pulled the anchor up and headed towards the sound. All of a sudden we were sailing amongst moored boats but I did not recognise any of them. Where were we? In Queenborough in Kent or somewhere like that?

Then the fog suddenly cleared and there we were in the upper part of Leigh harbour about two miles upstream of our finishing line with a foul tide to combat to get back to it. We started to sail back and met the other competitors coming the other way having finished the race. We were a bad last. The moral of this story is to never sail in bad visibility without a compass and don't rely on local knowledge, however good you think it might be.

Another race that stands out was completely different. This was in the pre-rescue boat days when the rule was that if a boat got into trouble then those fellow competitors that were nearest should render assistance. It was also when we sailed very long courses, one of the furthest points being the low-way buoy that marked the beginning of the Ray channel. It was here, not very far away from the scene of Simon's accident, that I managed to capsize in April, when the water was none too warm. The boat behind us stood by while we persuaded Crosswinds to stay upright, although we were unable to empty the water inside the boat (this was before the days of self-bailers).

The helmsman of the other boat then passed a towline and offered to tow us inshore. Since we had a following wind this went well with the crew clinging onto Crosswinds to prevent her falling over again. After a while, I pointed out a sandy beach and asked the other helmsman to let us go near it. Once ashore there, I believed that we could empty the water out and sail back to Leigh. But at this point a motorboat from another club arrived.

The two elderly gentlemen aboard announced they would take over and our saviour recovered his towline and departed. The motorboat took us in tow and headed for their home club's slipway and then it all began to go wrong. Now she was being towed at a different angle Crosswinds decided that she would prefer to travel on her side and did so several times despite our efforts to keep her upright. On one of these occasions the motorboat closing in to help knocked a hole in her bows. Then the rudder and tiller disappeared. Eventually the two old boys

'Crosswinds' alongside

Author's collection

decided that my crew member was 'all-in' and should go aboard the motorboat. He swam over and was hauled aboard but lost his glasses, which had so far stayed with him, in the process.

A few minutes later it was my turn and despite my protestations, I was hauled aboard. Crosswinds was then hauled unceremoniously on her side the rest of the way to the club slipway.

There we were well looked after. Other people put the boat away, while we were taken to the clubhouse, plied with strong drink and given dry clothing. The missing rudder and tiller were found and returned and a member of the club drove us home, assuring me that the boat could stay on their dinghy rack until repaired.

As it happened, a friend of mine was on holiday the next week and offered to repair the small hole in the bows and sail the boat back to Leigh if he could have the use of it for the rest of the week. This he did but unfortunately the weather did not permit him much sailing time.

Away events, such as Burnham Week and the biennial trip to the Norwich Frostbites continued. The former increased in popularity, at least with Leigh Sailing Club members, and there was a demand for accommodation. This was largely resolved by the hire of a large cottage, where Sally Setford presided as chief cook. Sally's culinary efforts were directed at one particular goal – a good performance in the week's farting contest that was held on the Thursday evening in one of the local clubs. To this end, we were fed large quantities of vegetables, largely leeks and cabbages, these being believed to enhance performance.

The inhabitants of the cottage were not solely male. One couple, who arrived at the last minute, were told that they could stay if they didn't mind sleeping on the settee in the lounge. One rather elderly inmate, on creeping downstairs in the middle of the night for a glass of water, was disgusted to find them fast asleep in the nude. But this was the Sixties and a more permissive age was dawning.

Although now a boat owner in my own right, for Burnham Week I preferred to crew on TEODs. On one occasion I was on the then star of the Leigh Sailing Club fleet, Mistral, TE 45. She was to have three different helmsmen for the week – Ron would sail her Monday to Thursday, Don on Friday and Graham, her normal helmsman, on Saturday. This was to fit in with their work commitments but us two crew members would remain unchanged.

The weather was typical of Burnham Week – bright sunshine and a fresh north-westerly wind. At that time TEODs and EODs were considered to be 'sea-going' yachts and sent on courses that took them well outside the River Crouch, perhaps round one of the buoys marking the Buxey sands. This meant a hard slog to windward followed by an alarming run in heavy seas back into the river.

One particular day the wind was slightly fresher than it had been so far and, sure enough, we were routed round the Inner Buxey buoy. Some boats, preferring discretion to valour, retired but the majority kept going. Just short of the turning mark, Mistral took an enormous sea aboard. The first thing that it hit was the after locker and it left us practically waterlogged. Somehow Ron persuaded the boat to stagger round the mark and we squared away on the run home. But the weight of water was making Mistral unstable and Ron told me to pump for my life. We were well back inside the river before the water was reduced to an acceptable level and I was able to look round.

We were lying last but one and, in an attempt to pass us the last boat had set a spinnaker, but this had merely blown to rags and they left it up, presumably because it was too dangerous for anyone to go onto the foredeck to take it down. I later heard that one of the EOD helmsmen was sailing with a dozen cans of beer in the boat's after locker, but with a teetotal crew. He admitted to being so scared on the run back that, as soon as the boat was in the comparatively quieter waters of the River Crouch, he drank the lot. Still all the boats returned safely, albeit many of them with minor damage.

By the Friday of this week, when Don was due to sail the boat, the brisk weather had taken its toll. The crews' hands were in a terrible state – we literally had blisters upon blisters. Although we had done our best with Elastoplast and other remedies our hands looked and felt terrible. When we assembled for the Friday race, the wind was blowing again fresh north-east. Don expressed doubt about the conditions. Carefully hiding our hands we stated that we were now used to them.

"Let's have a look at your hands," asked Don. Reluctantly we showed him.

"I'm not sailing with a crew in that state," he announced. So we had a relaxing day ashore.

The next day, the regular helmsman, Graham, turned up to sail the boat.

"What's this rubbish about not sailing yesterday?" he wanted to know, "A few blisters never hurt anyone."

Not only did we race that day, we won by a considerable margin. The second boat was a dot on the horizon as we finished. Admittedly conditions were much gentler, but Graham was not satisfied, as we only tied with the second EOD, despite their start of five minutes before us. Graham considered that we should have beaten all of them.

Some years later, I had a change from TEODs. The one I had agreed to crew on had a serious gear failure on the first day of Burnham Week and would not be racing in the near future. So I arranged to crew on a Royal Burnham One Design. These were a very different boat with a deep keel that enabled them to race in most conditions, if suitably reefed of course. They were more likely to break their masts than to capsize.

But this situation did not arise. We had two good days' sailing in gentle conditions, finishing near the front of a large fleet.

There was no room for me, however, on this boat on the fourth day. I was advised that if I wanted another sail on RBODs, I should board the Royal Burnham's trot boat and go round the fleet to see if anyone was short of a crew. These days, I would have known better, for it was definitely not a nice day, with heavy rain and very little wind.

However, I did find a crewing job on one of the less well-found RBODs. The owner had elected to sail as forward hand, while a friend of his, in whom he had every confidence, sailed the boat, although he had a damaged leg and walked with the aid of a stick. The helmsman's girl friend and myself made up the rest of the crew.

Our course took us up the River Roach, a tributary of the Crouch, and was sailed in heavy and persistent rain. But, just after we had rounded the buoy at the top of the river, the skies cleared and the wind freshened considerably. The run down to the Roach buoy started as a glorious sail, but we soon found that our spinnaker sheets could no longer be held in the hand and had to be cleated. At this point the TEOD ahead of us capsized. He insisted that he was all right as we swept past.

To my amazement, our helmsman announced his intention to gybe, with the spinnaker up, at the Roach buoy. It was noticeable that no other boats had set spinnakers and most were approaching the gybe with caution, as it is the tactic most likely to cause damage. But we gybed and there were two cracks as the spinnaker pole and the gooseneck holding the boom to the mast both broke. These were followed by a shout and a splash as the forward hand and owner slipped down the vertical foredeck into the water. The boat then skidded along on her side for a hundred yards or so, leaving the owner frantically swimming behind us. We then screwed up into the wind with the uncontrolled mainsail flapping and the knotted spinnaker billowing out to leeward. I hastily let the mainsail down.

We were in a sorry state. In addition to the damage, the helmsman was unable to move very far with his bad leg and had to comfort his girlfriend who was distraught. He did however tell me that there was an anchor and warp stowed under the foredeck so I anchored the boat in the hope that the owner would rejoin us, but after about ten minutes there was no sign of him. There was also no sign of any other boats from the considerable fleet that had largely been ahead of us.

The wind decreased slightly and we decided that we should attempt to return to Burnham. There was nothing to be done about the spinnaker other than to lash it as tightly as possible and hope that it would not pull us too far off course. We had a fair wind as far as the entrance to the River Roach at least and once in the main Crouch we might be able to obtain a tow. So, under foresail and knotted spinnaker we set off.

An easy enough sail took us down to the mouth of the Roach. This was a desolate sight. Boats of all descriptions littered the banks at the entrance, with most of the crews sitting on the seawalls. In the middle of the river an EOD lay awash with her mast broken into three sections. There was no sign of the crew who I knew well. But in the middle of this carnage there was still some racing going on. Some of our fellow Royal Burnhams were carrying on, reefed right down, with all four crew hanging out 'by their toenails'. Some EODs were also still racing, if it could be called that, for they were sailing the down-wind legs under bare poles and the windward legs under well-reefed jibs only. With the jib on a roller they could do this, while TEODs and similar vessels could not.

Our sail back to Burnham was a slow business but not as difficult as we had expected, for the wind had gone more southerly giving us a good slant up the river aided by a good tide. We made it almost to our mooring and a motor launch assisted us the last few yards. A large interested crowd watched us moor up, for although knotted spinnakers were not uncommon on the Crouch, ours was probably the most complex ever seen.

I never saw any of the crew again, but I did hear that the owner sailed back with the crew of a capsized Hornet that had been near the scene of our disaster. He expressed a desire to do the helmsman bodily harm, bad leg or no bad leg. Happily everybody else was OK, especially one TEOD that had ploughed up the north bank of the Crouch with full sail still set. The crew then stepped out, announcing their intention of going for a few beers.

With the introduction of the GP 14 and other plywood dinghies, there were more opportunities to sail 'away'. Every sailing or yacht club could put on an 'open meeting' for it's adopted class and invite entries from other clubs. There was also area and national championships held in different venues each year. Leigh Sailing Club has held the GP 14 area championship for London and the south east several times, but unfortunately the running of a national championship has proved logistically impossible for the club.

During the 1960s I took part in two national championships, one at Helensburgh in Scotland and the other at Torquay in Devon. I believe that I finished about 108th out of about 120 boats in both.

The Helensburgh event strained our survival techniques. Several of us slept in a caravan at Balloch on Loch Lomond which, we were assured was only a short drive from Helensburgh. In reality it was twenty-five minutes on a minor road that wound through hills and crossed Scottish braes. It was also peppered with warnings about cattle crossings. Not so funny after a day's sailing followed by an evening's drinking! (This was before the breathalyser, of course!)

Facilities on the sailing side were somewhat sparse. The boats were stored in a council car park and the adjoining public toilet had to be pressed into service as makeshift changing rooms, as the organising club had no clubhouse. The racing, as was normally the case with a championship, was started by a committee boat, which took up station about two miles away giving us a long sail before we even started. If we required refreshment after the race, snacks were provided, at inflated prices, from a tent pitched alongside the slipway. Alcohol, craved by many, could only be obtained by visiting a pub or hotel.

Added to this the weather was reasonably vile all week, only the practice race being sailed in benign conditions. Fairly typical was the race where I lost my balance when gybing the boat and then found myself unable to rise from the floorboards. Somehow my crew managed to keep the boat upright until we were able to stop, with all sails flapping, and investigate the problem. It turned out that the braces of my waterproof trousers, tied round my waist as they didn't function properly, had come adrift and the buckles had become lodged between the floorboards, restricting my ability to rise. We sorted this out and continued the race but shortly after this one of the Wembley boats tore past in a ball of spray with the crew shouting "Banzai!" After a further hundred yards they capsized, very messily, and at that point I decided that enough was enough, dropped the mainsail, retired from the race and returned to base.

Probably these sailing difficulties resulted to us having a very good time socially, although we had to adjust to certain local customs. We quickly found, for example, that if you ordered a cup of tea in a café you got just that. If you wanted milk in it you had to ask! Another big restriction was the Scottish licensing arrangements. Closing time was very early, 10pm. I believe, with no opening at all on Sunday evenings for public houses.

Our first evening in Helensburgh was fairly typical. Two LSC cadets helped me rig the boat in the car park and afterwards I invited them for a drink in the public bar department of the hotel opposite. We entered a bar that was empty apart from about eight large men behind a long counter. Feeling a bit apprehensive, I asked for three pints of best bitter and was advised that it was "verra strong". But we had it anyway and were soon joined by others from Leigh Sailing Club. Then the other customers began to arrive. All were holidaymakers from Glasgow and they started on the booze as though it was going out of fashion. Very quickly most were singing drunk, at least. Soon scuffles began to break out, hence the big barmen. We decided to go to the toilet in pairs, just in case.

But we survived and some of us repaired to a nearby fish and chip shop for something to eat before driving back to Balloch. We decided to eat our fish and chips out of the paper standing outside the shop. While we were there, a diminutive Scotsman, barely able to stand up, arrived and offered us each in turn "a bundle". We all declined and decided to finish our meal on the way back to Balloch, in case he summoned reinforcements. Later we learnt that we were lucky, since the fish and chip shop was the haunt of drunken Scotsmen wishing to have "a bundle" with the English sailors from the nearby submarine base at Faslane.

During the week there was intense rivalry between Leigh Sailing Club and Thorpe Bay Yacht Club, both on and off the water. Socially this took the form of playing tricks on each other – hiding one another's cars and so on. At the gathering on the penultimate night Thorpe Bay challenged Leigh to a game of rugby, to be played after the final race the next day. It was known that I had, at least, played rugby at school and I was roped in to play for Leigh as prop forward. In vain, I protested that my very limited experience of the game had been as a

A Swift catamaran

Author's collection

wing three-quarter. "With your weight you're a natural prop," I was told. The game was generally forecast to be a blood bath.

The weather the next day was not good and forecast to become a lot worse. Several of us decided that we could progress no further in the championship and repaired to a nearby tavern to play one another at darts instead of having what promised to be a rough sail. We had not been playing long when several ratings from Faslane came in and suggested that we have a darts match of Navy versus yachtsmen. What we did not immediately realise was that this match was for pints, the loser of each game to buy his opponent a beer. Soon a first class party was under way. On about the fourth pint I remembered the rugby match.

This had a sobering effect and after a while those involved felt we had better have a look at the sailing to see if the race was about to end. As we came within sight of the water, a scene of carnage was revealed. Several boats were capsized with the crews trying to right them. Others with broken masts and other damaged gear were being towed in. Very few boats had finished a shortened race. In the circumstances, much to my relief, nobody felt like playing rugby.

The event concluded with the prize giving at the Town Hall. There was speculation as to what, exactly, this would consist of. On arrival we were all presented with a free glass of scotch. So far, so good. But there didn't seem to be any chance of refill, either free or purchased. On the stage stood a table containing the trophies, which were the property of our class association. Also on the table was a shoebox and speculation was rife as to what it contained. The consensus of opinion was that it was envelopes containing cash prizes.

When the prize giving started, the wife of the Provost of Helensburgh presented the trophies, but the shoebox remained undisturbed. At the very end, the mystery was solved. The commodore of the host club made a speech, thanking the Lady Provost. He then opened the shoebox and produced a single rose which he said had been 'especially cultivated by the parks superintendent' and presented her with it. After the official party had departed, a gentleman appeared on the stage with a dozen haggis's and, after explaining that he was sorry that he had not got one for everyone, threw them into the crowd.

The weather was still terrible and one of the Leigh Sailing Club party expressed a dread that it might delay our departure the next day. But we went anyway and braved a series of thunderstorms through Scotland and the Lake District.

Undeterred, we went to the championships at Torquay the following year and it was all very different. We took two boats, one on top of another, on an adapted trailer behind a car and drove through the night, arriving at Torquay in time for breakfast. Accommodation was in a pub on the sea front, a short walk from the host club and the dinghy park.

The club itself was a very long established one and its attitude was typified by a group of business men who used to gather on its balcony in fine weather. They would position themselves so that the steward could see them from behind the bar. Every now and again one of them would raise a finger and the steward would appear with another round of drinks for them, complete with the change for a five pound note, for he knew that this would be the payment. While I was there, I witnessed the introduction of a new club secretary – Wing Commander X was taking over from Lieutenant Colonel Y.

We found all of this somewhat daunting and wondered why such a superior club had taken on a meeting of small dinghies – surely they would be better suited with an event for some premier class, such as Dragons? We came to the conclusion that they must have been inspired by a combination of money and prestige.

The sailing was in Tor Bay with launching from concrete slipways, probably of wartime origin, in Torquay harbour. One of these came near to causing trouble. As crew I had a young nurse whose sailing experience, at least in GP 14s, was small. During one race, in which we were already nearly last, she put the spinnaker up upside down. I decided that this would be a good moment to retire and gave her the helm while I sorted the spinnaker out. It was low tide as we approached the slipway and I jumped out forrard into about six inches of water. But the nurse, wishing to be helpful, jumped out aft into about thirty feet of water, since we were on the very end of the slipway. Fortunately she took it well.

The big difference with Helensburgh was the prizes. The winner received a complete cine kit – camera, projector, etc. With the rest of prize winners receiving substantial gifts as well as the class trophies. After this some of the brighter sparks decided to liven up the host club.

I last saw them, dressed in the bunting that had earlier decorated the clubhouse, bouncing up and down to the Beatles' Yellow Submarine on the billiard table in about two inches of beer.

After some years of attending national championships, the Leigh Sailing Club GP 14s were rewarded when Sally Setford, crewed by Mike Fitzpatrick won the nationals when they were held at nearby Thorpe Bay. Since then the club has won several other major events, including the Mirror Dinghy National and World Championships.

As a change from GP 14s, I sometimes crewed on Swift catamarans. One notable event was a week at Whitstable in Kent. Here we lived onboard a borrowed cruiser in Whitstable harbour and sailed the Swift from the beach. It blew reasonably hard all week, so hard on one day that spray was carried over the harbour wall from outside. Needless to say racing was cancelled that day, but not on the others when it was still very fresh. How my helmsman, Brian, found his way round the courses I do not know, since I was blinded by spray for most of each race. We won every race bar one, in which we were second. Inevitably, the day we were due to sail back to Leigh was a flat calm and we had to travel back by train, abandoning some of our gear on the cruiser so that we could fill one of our bags with the prizes we had won.

THE LIGHTERAGE TRADE

Meanwhile, back at the Port of London, I had had a job change within the dues office at West India Dock, becoming the lighterage dues clerk and this position needs a little historical explanation.

Before there were any enclosed docks, lightermen and watermen used to collect their cargoes direct from ships moored in the river. This was, of course, free of charge, but there were ample opportunities for dishonesty and crime became rife with lightermen as involved as any others. Eventually the enclosed docks came into being and the crime rate fell considerably.

However, the powerful watermen's lobby resisted attempts by the new dock companies to charge them for entering the docks, stating that they had always had the right to receive and deliver goods without charge. They won the day and their rights were embodied in what was called the Free Water Clause. The right of free access was extended to vessels trading to London from inside the port area, i.e. inside a line from Walton-on-the-Naze to the North Foreland, including Colchester, Maldon, Whitstable and the rivers Medway and Swale. It is said that this was a reward to these ports for continuing to supply London during the Great Plague.

This, then, was the situation inherited by the PLA when the authority took over from the private dock companies in 1909. However, it was quickly obvious that the docks were being used as a parking place for lighters for which there was currently no work. Much congestion was caused and it was often difficult for a ship with its attendant tugs to pick its way through masses of drifting lighters to its berth. Surrey Docks, where much timber was handled, were particularly bad with rafted timber adding to the congestion. So bad, in fact, that sailing barges could often only move around by taking a wire ashore and winding up on it, which was very hard work for the crew when they wished to move from one end of a dock to the other.

Something had to be done and a system of penalties was brought in to discourage over-long stays. These were administered by the dues office in each dock and were described under 'heads'.

In my time they were: -

Dues Head I: For entering and leaving the dock without working – 1/- per net ton.

Dues Head II: For entering the dock more than two tides before the arrival of the ship containing the cargo consigned to the craft – 9d per net ton.

Dues Head III: For leaving the dock more than three tides after receiving or discharging cargo – 9d per net ton.

Dues Head IV: For arriving more than two tides before the designated ship broke bulk (started to discharge cargo.)

Rent could also be charged in the event of a long stay in dock.

No doubt there was a good reason for the difference in the number of tides that led to the imposition of dues, but it escapes me. The prime documents for the assessment of these dues were the docking note made out by each lighterman as his craft locked in and the pass releasing goods from the docks.

The docking note included the name of the lighter, her net tonnage, her owners and the ship for which she was bound. This last was all-important and, if it was omitted, a charge of 10/6 for 'docking note informality' could be raised. The net tonnage was often inaccurate and frequently left off but this did not matter since tonnages were checked against the PLA Craft Registration book, if required.

Lighterage firms were allowed to inspect docking notes within twenty-four hours of their lighters' arrival. Most of the larger firms took advantage of this and their docking notes were put to one side until it was done. Transfers between ships were allowed and transfer forms were often lodged at the same time.

All these measures were designed to reduce congestion within the docks and were, at least, partially successful, since many of the lighterage companies set up 'roads' in the river where spare lighters could be left. 'Roads' were looked after by a 'roadsman' whose base was often a shed, or even an old railway coach, perched on one of the collar barges that were permanently secured to the moorings of the 'roads'. However, it was often still possible to walk across the docks on the massed lighters that were drifting around.

It was the job of the lighterage dues clerk to control the dues on lighters. Each day a bag was received from the dockmaster's department containing the documentation for the previous day. This included the dockmaster's report which detailed all shipping movements, a declaration of each ship entering the dock, together with towage orders for any tugs used, a craft report detailing the lighters that had entered and left the dock, together with docking notes for those that had arrived and passes for those that had left with cargo. In the case of West India Dock there was a separate set of documents for the Blackwall entrance which dealt almost exclusively with lighters and other 'small fry', and yet another for the remote East India Dock.

The lighterage dues clerk would open the bag and sort out the contents, passing anything to do with actual ships to the ship dues clerk. The docking notes were then sorted, with those likely to be examined by lighterage company representatives put to one side and the rest filed alphabetically under the lighters' names. Docking notes for those leaving were then extracted, married with the passes and examined in case dues of any kind had been incurred. Around five per cent did and bills were then sent to the lighterage companies involved.

None of the lighterage companies liked receiving bills and would do their damnedest to wriggle out of paying unless, of course, their customer was prepared to pay. The best example of this was a fog, particularly one occurring at a weekend and there were plenty of these during the 1950s. On the Friday lighters would enter the dock anticipating the arrival of their designated ships over the weekend. If the ships had not arrived by the second tide on the Monday, all of these craft would incur dues and bills would be dispatched to the lighterage companies. Over the next few days they would all return, accompanied by pleas mentioning 'acts of God', poverty, etc. The whole lot would then be submitted to the charges office at head office for a ruling. Inevitably the charges would either be given up or reduced by fifty percent, depending on the severity of the fog. Then a credit note would have to be prepared for each one. The games people play!

Some unusual events occurred involving dues. A motor barge, the Clenwood, called in and left some days later without working, apparently because of a crew shortage. Another motor barge, owned by one of the former sailing barge companies, was the subject of a very complex situation, the details of which I forget, which resulted in a dues bill. After two lengthy telephone calls from the manager of the company, I gave up and referred the matter to Mr. Jones of the charges office. The manager was claiming that the dues should be assessed a different way which would save his company the grand sum of 1/4d. This, I felt, was a matter of policy that only head office could solve.

Mr. Jones had earlier been head of the tonnage dues office at Tilbury Docks for many years and what he didn't know about dues charges wasn't worth knowing. He had about an hour's conversation with the barge company manager who refused to back down. Jones then suggested that since his office was quite near our head office, that the manager came over to see him. A further long argument then ensued during the meeting until Jones, in exasperation, offered the man 1/4d out of his own pocket. This was politely refused and the manager agreed to accept our version of the charge, under protest. The matter was never properly resolved.

Another charge that caused much heartache was a fee for mooring a drifting lighter. Given the normal level of drifting lighters, this charge could have been rendering hundreds of times a week, but it was only submitted occasionally, probably when there was an insurance matter involved. Usually such bills were returned with a covering letter stating something like: "A PLA employee was seen near the lighter just before it was cast adrift. We can only assume that it was he who untied the lighter, probably for a good reason, but, under the circumstances we feel your charge should be withdrawn." Yet another matter for the charges office!

Loose lighters did present a problem, although at West India and Millwall Docks it was comparatively mild compared with the congestion at Surrey Docks where the problem was compounded by large quantities of floating timber. And yet the biggest drift of them all occurred just outside West India Dock. The dock was exceptionally busy and there were enough ships using the main lock for all lighters to be routed through the Blackwall entrance. More ships naturally meant more lighters and by the time the Blackwall entrance closed for the night there were 200-300 still waiting to come in. Despite the fact that they were only held by the headfast (bow rope) of the leading one, they were left unattended. During the night the wind got up and the headfast could take the strain no longer. A huge number of lighters went adrift on the Thames, gradually splitting into smaller groups as further ropes broke.

Soon there were lighters everywhere. They drifted onto wharves, fouled roads of other lighters, ran onto the slipways of barge repairers and parked themselves on unoccupied stretches of foreshore. They represented a considerable menace to navigation and the Thames Navigation Service issued a plea for any tug under way on the river to assist in rounding them up. The rescuers must have done a good job for, by working hours next day there was little sign that anything had happened. So far as I know only minimal damage was done.

It is often believed that the PLA ran the docks completely, but this was far from the case. Many services were provided by private enterprise including stevedoring, cargo superintendence, ship repairing, ship towage and, of course, lighterage. At one time any experienced lighterman with capital could buy a few lighters and set up in business as a lighterage contractor. At the time that I became involved most lighterage firms were converting from being family concerns or partnerships to limited companies. This, I heard, was due to one family firm being crippled by death duties on the demise of the founder and, despite being prosperous with some good contracts, having to be taken over by a larger firm. Indeed the lighterage industry was a hotchpotch ranging from large firms with about 400 employees to a widow with only a couple of men to handle her late husband's business. Some of the larger firms had other interests, often in the wharves they served or in the commodities that they carried, while others were part of large companies in the transport business.

The bigger the company, the bigger the local organisation. The largest lighterage companies kept a foreman in each of the London docks, very often supported by an assistant or 'runner' (It is believed that these gentlemen were, at one time, expected to literally run from the docks to the City with information.) A smaller company would have one or two foremen who would visit the docks in turn. Others, usually those whose headquarters were at a distance, would rely on the post or get individual lightermen to visit the dues office.

As I have mentioned earlier representatives of lighterage firms could visit the office to change docking notes or to lodge transfer documents. Certain foremen or their runners were regular visitors but none as much as Harry who represented the biggest firm of all, the Thames Steam Tug & Lighterage Co. Ltd, known the length of the river as 'Limited'.

Every morning, almost without fail, he was waiting for me when I arrived at nine o'clock. Nothing ever stopped him, despite the fact that he must have been at least seventy years old, not bad weather, strikes or sickness. He would sit quietly smoking until I presented him with the previous days' docking notes for his craft, which would be numerous. Then he would work his way through them altering names and adding transfer forms where appropriate. Only when this work was completed could he, if his time permitted, be persuaded to yarn about life on the river. To my great regret, I have forgotten most of what he told me.

At lunchtime I would often get a visit from Harry's 'runner' who he always referred to as 'young Con', although they must have been of a similar age. Con would ask to see a number of docking notes that he would alter or add a transfer document to. Harry, on his next visit, would ask to see Con's lunchtime work and, sighing deeply, would alter it all, often back to the original saying something like: "That's the trouble with these youngsters – they thinks they knows."

At one time Harry became concerned about my travelling arrangements. He was amazed that I came all the way from Leigh-on-Sea by train and was then faced with the long walk from Stepney East Station. Like the majority of employees in the docks, he probably lived somewhere close by like Plaistow or Custom House. He mentioned that his firm kept a small tug or 'tosher' in the dock, which was usually at the Crosswall just inside the dock early in the morning. Why didn't I contact the tug and get a lift through the dock? If I told the skipper that Harry said it would all right then there would be no objections. But I could think of a number – suppose the tug wasn't there and I wasted time looking for it? Or it wasn't ready to depart? And if it were dirty then my suit would suffer. So I never took Harry's kind offer up – again much to my later regret.

If Harry took leave or went sick – both very rare events – then his replacement would be the firm's London dock foreman who was a very different character. He had the appearance of a funeral director and was the only person in the docks known to wear a wing collar. Rumour suggested that he was a lay preacher in his spare time and he certainly looked the part. Con was, of course, extremely disappointed that he was not allowed to stand in for Harry and did his best to undermine the relief. But the man was no fool and quickly had Con's measure.

Characters also existed at a higher level in the lighterage business and, rather surprisingly in a male dominated trade, one of these was a woman, Dorothea Woodward-Fisher, a very formidable lady indeed. I never met her, for my wars with her were over the telephone, but I have seen photos and the rumours were true, she really did sport a monocle and cigarette holder!

Her husband had started in the usual small way, acquiring a few redundant lighters and building upon this to create a sizeable business. By my time Dorothea was running at least the office side of the business, if not all of it. We had many verbal sparring matches and I came to dread the words "Mrs Woodward-Fisher on the phone for you." But she was a shrewd businesswoman and eventually kept her firm running long after others would have given up. She also did much charitable work and the Poplar, Blackwall & District Rowing Club owes much of its success to her.

At Christmas the lighterage companies distributed largesse, largely in the shape of office stationery – diaries, pencils, rulers and especially calendars. Nearly every lighterage firm on the river produced their own calendar and usually they consisted of a tide table for the coming year

Lighterage tug 'Vange' with tow of lighters

S. Emery collection

149

'Friston Down'
S. Emery collection

A launch type tug or 'tosher'
S. Emery collection

surmounted by a picture, often of one of their tugs. We found them very useful as we worked with tides, but after the dues office staff had had one each, there was often another twenty-seven or so left. These were distributed to other offices or taken home in batches, probably to be sent as Christmas presents to remote relatives.

One day about the end of November a lighterage foreman said to me casually: "Wait till you see Fielder Hickman's calendar." (Fielders being one of the smaller lighterage concerns) Thereafter a succession of foremen mentioned the calendar, the descriptions becoming more and more lurid. A typical one was: "You know that Pirelli calendar with all them naked girls? Well Fielders' one is better."

A few days before Christmas Fielders' foreman, a taciturn individual, arrived and threw a large envelope on to my desk. "Calendar", he said, not being one to waste words. After he had gone the staff gathered round while I opened the envelope. Strangely a couple of lighterage foremen joined the throng from somewhere. From the envelope I drew out a large calendar which displayed a wonderful picture ... of York Minster! Everyone collapsed with laughter – I had been the subject of a well-concerted 'wind-up'.

Another source of merriment was the interpretation of ship's names on docking notes by lightermen. Not much could go wrong with names such as Adviser or City of York (to name but two of the regulars) but a ship of say Russian or Greek nationality could have many versions of its name appear. Sometimes the lighterman would just give up and put 'Russian ship' or leave the space blank and this was why corrections were permitted. Strangely our own typist who translated Kirsten Smits as Thirteen Suits committed one of the best blunders over a ship's name.

However there was sometimes a serious side to name alteration. Once a foreman asked me for a certain docking note although, strictly speaking, he was too late. He explained that the lighterman who had made it out was losing his sight and if the firm had to pay a charge on the lighter, he might be found out and lose his job. Of course I allowed him to alter it, but I doubt that the foreman could cover up for the lighterman forever.

Most lighterage firms of any size had their own tugs. Those that did not relied on various towage contractors to tow their craft. By the 1950s the time honoured rowing or 'driving' of lighters was hardly ever seen. Tugs were allowed in to the docks on the understanding that they only towed craft belonging to their owners and did not ply for hire. They also had to leave by the next tide.

This last restriction normally presented no difficulty, except once. One of the largest owners sent one of its tugs into West India Dock to tow out a batch of loaded lighters. This tug broke down and was beyond local repair so on the next tide a second tug was despatched to tow out the first one plus the lighters. The second tug managed to lose its propeller within the dock. The owners were fast running out of tugs but eventually a third one entered the dock and managed to remove everything. It was decided that this situation was without precedent and that no charge should be rendered. This decision was probably taken after consulting the book of 'precedents' and head office instructions with its Shakespearean admonition.

Lighterage tugs fell into two main classes. These were the large tugs that handled most of the river traffic and were mainly diesel powered with a crew of four, and the launch type tugs also diesel powered with two crew members. Because of their relatively small size this latter class was, together with small ships, referred to as 'toshers'. They largely operated within the docks or on the several canals leading from the docks. This was not an exclusive rule and some 'toshers' operated well enough on the tideway. Indeed some lighterage firms only had a 'tosher'.

The differences in the two classes were not reflected in sound. The siren of Friston Down, one of the largest lighterage tugs emitted only a funny little squeak while some of the toshers could produce a deep-throated roar.

All lightermen as part of their long apprenticeship had to know how to row or 'drive' a lighter and also how the currents ran on the river, which arches of the London bridges were the most favourable and so on. But all this was in danger of becoming a lost art because of the reliance on tugs until there was a strike of tug crews. This was over a proposal by the employers to reduce the number of crew on the larger tugs from four (skipper, mate, engineer and boy) to three by the elimination of the boy. The crews regarded this as a retrograde step since the boy largely functioned as cook. But, more seriously, tug boy was regarded as the first step on the ladder to fully-fledged lighterman and, perhaps, tug skipper.

The employers, too, were alarmed for they were faced with the prospect of a large force of lightermen with little to do, but still on pay.

It was felt that since lightermen still had the skills, if not the practice, the old methods of driving, etc. must be reintroduced. However there was one big snag. Most of the large oars used for driving had been scrapped, largely by burning. A large-scale search then ensued for any survivors. Every storage shed, barge yard or other likely hiding place was ransacked in the hopes of finding a few of the oars. Even I was asked if I had seen any in the dock.

At West India Dock lighterage movement virtually dried up, although lighters already docked could still be worked. The situation was, I suspect, compounded by a desire by the ordinary lightermen to support their chums on the tugs but, after a couple of days a few lighters did arrive propelled by manpower. Fortunately, unlike many dock strikes, this one was quickly settled and did not reoccur. I am pleased to report that the old skill of driving has since been revived in the shape of annual races with heavy lighters again being rowed by men.

For an annual fee, some of the larger lighterage firms could keep a small tug within the dock to tow their own craft. Otherwise lighter movement was by sheer brute strength with a lightermen hauling on the headfast or bow rope. They reckoned once the bulk of the lighter was moving then its momentum made the job easier. With a fair wind it was possible for a lighterman to shift a lighter across the docks by holding his coat open as a small sail. Or there was towage from the PLA's own 'tosher', the one in West India Dock being named Plashy.

This tug was mainly kept for the towage of the PLA's own lighters and those of our two lighterage contractors, W. J. R. Whitehair and the General Lighterage Co. but she did occasionally tow other craft. One of my jobs was to vet her log sheets to pick up the odd instance of her performing such a tow and bill the company involved.

Her daily routine usually consisted of 'starting engine' followed by a little gentle towage of PLA craft, if required, lunch, a little more towage, perhaps and then securing for the night. Most of the remaining time, particularly immediately before lunch and 'securing' was described as 'seeking', this being the term used when a tug was looking for work in the shape of tows. Cynically, I believed it to also be a euphemism for a long lunch-hour in the pub or an early departure for home – but I may have been wrong.

Eventually I moved to a different job within the office, the preparation of loading and discharging accounts, but I still kept an eye on the lighterage situation. In some ways it was deteriorating, as lighterage companies merged or wiped out their subsidiaries to present a more streamlined image. Thames Steam Tug merged with the General Lighterage Company and younger men replaced Harry and Con.

But it was an extremely busy period for the lighterage trade, especially for the Surrey Docks that specialised in the import of timber. There were a number of firms which had no work of their own but made their money by hiring lighters to others who needed more craft. But even they ran out of spare craft. The main lighterage companies resorted to borrowing from each other, where possible. Eventually the wharves to which cargo was destined could not cope and loaded lighters were moored to buoys within the docks (at a price).

But this was a last flurry and by the time I departed in 1964 for the allegedly exalted post of an executive officer at head office the

'Redoubtable' and others awaiting grain cargo

Author's collection

'Cambria', the last barge to trade commercially under sail

Author's collection

lighterage trade was on the decline. For a time there was some hope with a new trade – the handling of LASH cargoes, an acronym for 'lighter aboard ship' which entailed floating containers being launched from specialised ships and then towed to their ultimate destinations under the control of lightermen. But the Thames lighter generally did not lend itself to the carriage of containers and as general cargo ships declined so did lighterage with further amalgamations and some of the smaller companies closing when shift work was introduced. "Unreasonable money for unreasonable hours," the owner of one small company declared when announcing the closure of his business.

Many lightermen, too young or unwilling to take voluntary severance, were regraded as dockers. This came hard to them as they were used to a degree of independence and had served a long apprenticeship to acquire their skills on the water. Now they had to learn a new set of skills that was alien to them. Most left at the first opportunity.

In 1990 the last mercantile lighterage company, Braithwaite & Dean, announced its withdrawal from general lighterage to concentrate on the

Sailing barge 'Hydrogen' with reduced rig as her sailingdays came to an end

Author's collection

carriage of building materials for enterprises such as Canary Wharf and this type of work plus the carriage of London's rubbish and the operation of pleasure cruises is all that is left. The lighterage trade has followed the sailing barges that it partially replaced in to oblivion but without the leisure revival that has resurrected the barges.

By the end of the 1950s there were few sailing barges trading under sail. During this decade the last fleet of any size had come to an end. These were the powder barges of Wood's of Gravesend, which had been kept together since it was believed to be hazardous to carry explosives in powered vessels. Once a way was found to do this Wood's sailormen were redundant and were sold off, several of them becoming yachts.

By 1959 only Cambria was trading fully under sail but there were also a few others in lighterage work in the Ipswich area. A handful was still operating under auxiliary power with reduced sail. These included Horlock's Redoubtable and Remercie which were frequent visitors to West India Dock, and Sully's Beatrice Maud which I remember in West India Dock with a large sailing catamaran on deck. A few units of the London & Rochester Trading Company still carried sail of some sort, but this company had built up a large fleet of motor barges, many of them former sailing barges but an increasing number were custom built and the earlier ones were derided by the nick-name 'Spam Cans'.

There were also the barges retained to compete in the annual barge matches – Everards' Sara, Veronica and Dreadnought and London & Rochester's Sirdar.

The Thames Match, which had been sailed almost up to the outbreak of World War II, was revived in 1953 to celebrate the Coronation. It was originally intended to be a 'one off' event and was organised as a joint venture between the Thames and Medway barge match committees. It was a race for commercial craft only (no barge yachts), although it did include a class for vessels with auxiliary power. The main competition was between Everards' Sara and the London and Rochester Trading Co.'s Sirdar in the Bowsprit Class. It was a successful event and it was decided to make it an annual competition. The Medway Match was revived in 1965 and in this year Everards restored their famous racing barge Veronica. She had not been active for some years but was allowable by the rule that competitors must have 'a clean swept hold' that kept yacht barges out of the matches until 1959.

In 1963 Everards announced their intention to withdraw from the barge matches and break up their barges. This left Sirdar with no realistic competition and she was employed by her owners on promotional work until 1972 when she was hulked at Bedlam's Bottom on the Medway where Veronica, which had been reprieved and spent a few years as a houseboat under a different name, later joined her.

But by this time the barge matches had become even more popular. In 1962 the Blackwater Match had been revived and a new match added on the River Orwell. 1964 saw a revival at Southend, also considered to be a partial replacement for the Thames Match that had been discontinued after the demise of Everards' and Wood's fleets. Since then the Colne Match (1972), the Swale Match (1973) and a passage race from Gravesend to the Orwell have all been added. The Thames Match was revived again for the 1975 Clipper Regatta and, in the last few years, has once again become a regular fixture. All of these matches are now contested by a fleet consisting entirely of converted

A 'Spam can'

Author's collection

158

craft, none of which are used for carrying cargo, although one of their number, Edme is scheduled to carry freight again.

In 1960 two well-known names in the barge trade – Francis & Gilders of Colchester and Daniels Bros. of Whitstable – disappeared when their parent company lost the tax advantage of running them as separate entities. Indeed this change led to the demise of several lighterage companies that were also subsidiaries of larger firms. Even those sailing barge hulls cut down to power only had not long to go, as traditional trades declined or were swapped to container or road transport, leaving what remained to the more recently built motor vessels, which themselves declined almost to extinction by the 1990s.

But help was just around the corner for the sailing barge that by the mid-1960s was much in demand as a yacht or charter vessel. Many that had been reduced to a motor barge or bare hulk were reigned for a further lease of life and the supporting trades of sail maker, barge builder, shipwright, etc. were revived to support them. The barge matches in which they used to compete for annual trophies have been revived, and even expanded and, all being well, the Thames barge should sail on well into the 21st Century.

Racing barge 'Sara'

Author's collection

'Veronica' with full sail

Author's collection

At anchor after a Barge Match

Author's collection

THE DOCKMASTER'S DEPARTMENT

The tonnage dues office worked closely with the dockmaster's department, which was led by the dockmaster who ranked only after the superintendent and chief engineer in the hierarchy of the dock. The department was very maritime in its organisation with watches being worked, as at sea, times kept on the twenty-four hour system and a distinctly sea-going feel to its structure.

Under the dockmaster was a senior assistant dockmaster who acted as a deputy and there were the assistant dockmasters, one in charge of each watch with, in the case of West India Dock, an extra set to look after East India Dock plus one to keep an eye on the Blackwall entrance which worked day work purely on the entry and exit of tugs and lighters.

All dockmasters had to be former seagoing officers holding an Extra Master's Ticket (Merchant Navy) or its Royal Navy equivalent. They were also require to 'live on the job' because of their shift duties and were each provided with a house for themselves and their families close to the lock side of their dock. Combined with a reasonable salary, this was a tempting proposition for any officer who wished to 'come ashore' to be with a growing family.

Under each assistant dockmaster the watch would consist of a lock foreman, his assistant and about a dozen lockmen. These would be responsible for operating the lock machinery and for manual fine adjustments to a ship in or entering the lock (tugs could only do so much). Bridgemen were also drawn from the ranks of the lockmen and each would be responsible for a bridge over one of the cuttings within the dock, opening for shipping as required and stopping road and rail traffic.

In his excellent book about life on motor barges after the war, 'Punching the Tide', Captain Duncan Francis mentions the difficulties of attracting the attention of bridgemen to swing bridges for small craft. He believes that their attitude was largely responsible for the initials 'PLA' being taken to stand for 'Please Leave Alone' among waterborne folk. He is probably right!

I had only one experience of a bridgeman's indiscretions and that was very much third hand in the shape of an insurance claim that happened to pass through the dues office. At the time the method of stopping traffic while shipping passed through a bridge was for the bridgeman to pull down a large wooden beam boldly painted in red and white stripes to block entry to the bridge by vehicles. The beam had a counter balance so that if the rope was released it would spring upright, opening the road.

In this instance, the bridgeman had opened the road by releasing the rope but had left the fall of the rope lying in the road. The rope became entangled round the back axle of a lorry and, as it tightened, the beam was pulled down on to the bonnet of a following car, badly denting the bonnet and smashing the windscreen. The occupant of the car was injured. Unfortunately he was a commercial traveller who knew all about insurance claims.

Craft locking in to one of the London Docks

Author's collection

163

He threw the book at the PLA, claiming for loss of earnings, stress and all sorts of other things. The PLA, or at least their insurers, had to pay up and shortly afterwards the wooden beams were replaced with gates.

To return to the manning of the dockmaster's department, each watch also included a booking foreman, his assistant and a transport foreman. The booking foreman kept the records (dockmaster's reports, etc.) while his assistant did the physical bit of jumping around lighters and other craft handing out and collecting docking notes and so on.

What the transport foreman actually did was obscure. He was provided with a bicycle and would cycle round the dock to meet an incoming ship on its berth. There he was expected to complete any necessary paperwork in conjunction with the representative of the ship's agent. In actual fact he very often ended up working for the dock pilot.

Most ships entering the London docks had to take three pilots – a sea pilot from the Channel to Gravesend, a river pilot from Gravesend to the entrance lock of whichever of the enclosed docks she was bound for and a dock pilot from there to her berth. Dock pilots were highly experienced watermen who piloted ships of the regular users of the dock. One would have, say, the contract to pilot all the ships of the Harrison Line that called at West India Dock from the West Indies on a regular basis. Dock pilots could charge virtually what they liked for their services and this accounted for the several smart motor cruisers stowed in odd corners of the docks; dock pilots owned them all! The situation of a ship having to take three pilots was however farcical, especially in the case of ships bound for Tilbury Docks. They would exchange a sea pilot for a river pilot just to navigate a few hundred yards to the entrance to Tilbury.

The dock pilot was responsible for the mooring of a ship on its berth and was supposed to employ a gang of men to handle the ropes and wires involved. But often the transport foreman would be in the dock pilot's pocket. Arriving early at the berth he would collect up any bystanders (usually dockers) and offer them small sums of money to take the ropes, etc. Later he would be reimbursed and collect his own fee from the pilot.

There was three office staff at the dockmasters department. The actual dockmaster's clerk we saw but rarely, possibly because he was busy studying for accountancy exams (indeed he later became chief accountant of the Royal Docks). The writer under him was also seldom seen for reasons that will become apparent. Our main dealings were with number three, an assistant foreman whose demeanour originally caused us dues office staff to unfairly give him the nickname 'The Cretin'. In actual fact he was highly intelligent and hard working and was in the dockmasters department because he was about the only assistant foreman in West India Dock who did not wish to work overtime, something of a rare occurrence in the dockmaster's office.

Finally there was Albert. He referred to himself as the dockmaster's foreman and seemed to be some sort of warrant officer between the dockmasters and the lockside staff. What his actual duties were meant to be remains a mystery. I can only surmise that they were public relations since his day seemed to consist of visiting contacts of the dockmaster (including the dues office) and yarning while drinking vast quantities of tea if nothing stronger was available.

Albert had his moment of glory. There was, at that time, a radio programme called "Down your Way" whose host, Franklin Engleman, used to visit places of interest, interview the more lively inhabitants and finally play their favourite piece of music.

The programme visited the Isle of Dogs (including West India & Millwall Docks) and Albert was selected to be interviewed. When asked to select his piece of music, he replied: "I dunno. Tell yer what. I 'ave some o' that 'Andels lager and lime." Sadly round about the time I left the Dock, Albert died in office. He was not replaced.

There were those in the dock who likened the dockmaster of the time (who we will call Captain Fraser) to Captain Bligh of Bounty fame. This was grossly unfair because Bligh was not all that bad. The good captain certainly liked to act the bluff sea dog or perhaps 'Bucko Mate' is more accurate. One of his pet hates, with good reason, was the drifting lighters within the dock. Captain Fraser considered that all lighters should be moored fore and aft in neat lines while awaiting cargo. Periodically he would arrange a meeting with representatives of the lighterage trade who would patiently explain the impracticability of his suggestion. The meetings inevitably ended in farce and everybody continued to leave lighters lying around. Until the next time, for the captain would not give up.

Like all the dockmasters, Captain Fraser lived in a PLA house near the lockside, albeit a somewhat grander one than his underlings, with his wife who was known to all as 'Olive Oil' (though I don't remember the captain ever being referred to as Popeye). And this accounted for the second member of the staff of the dockmaster's office, for he was employed for much of his time in running errands for Olive. His reward was to come in every Sunday to deal with the men's timesheets for which he received a complete Sunday's overtime for a couple of hours work.

All dockmasters were given the honorary title of captain. One day when Fraser had been making himself particularly obnoxious towards the staff of the dues office, one of them approached me and asked what the correct term of address was for a second mate in the Merchant Navy. I replied that it was "Sir" from underlings and "Mister" from those equal to or above him. I was intrigued as to why he wanted to know this, as he was not normally interested in maritime matters. He told me that, somehow or the other, he had found that although our dockmaster was in possession of the necessary Extra Master's Certificate, the highest that he had risen in the Merchant Navy was second mate. He now intended to put this information to good use.

He rang the dockmaster's department and asked for "Mr. Fraser". A somewhat surprised Albert put him through to the great man. My colleague then gave the captain some information that he had asked for earlier in the day, periodically addressing him as "Mr. Fraser". Sounds of apoplexy could be heard from the phone could be heard across the room. Eventually he finished the conversation wished "Mr. Fraser" good day and hung up. The good captain was, by then, apparently speechless. Strangely there were no reprisals and Fraser always treated my colleague with respect from then on. Albert's comment was that someone needed to stand up to him.

They could certainly have some fun and games at the dockmaster's. One night the lock foreman was virtually on his own, the assistant dockmaster had disappeared somewhere and most of the others were either playing cards or catching up on their sleep in the lockmen's cabin. No ships were expected, either in or out. But the foreman became aware of a medium sized coaster about to moor up to the pier head, normal procedure for a ship about to enter the dock.

"Where you for?" he hailed it.

"Timber Wharves, plis," came the reply.

And this proved to be the extent of the crew's English. But all seemed to be well, as Montague Meyer , the timber company had a wharf at the end of Millwall Dock known as Timber Wharves. So the foreman locked the ship in and thought no more of it after he had done his best to convey to the crew how to get to Meyer's place. The ship wasn't big enough to warrant a dock pilot so they were on their own and would probably have a job to rouse the bridgemen on the two intervening bridges.

Some time later the phone rang. It was the night watchman at Meyer's.

"Why did you send us this ship?" he asked," We ain't expectin' nothin'."

There was some frantic searching of the ships expected list. But this one was not mentioned – the smaller ones often were not. In the end the foreman told the night watchman to send the ship back. When it arrived he moored it just inside the lock as a problem to be sorted out in the morning.

Next morning various people tried their linguistic skills on the ship's crew and eventually picked up something that sound like the name of a small but well-known firm of ship's agents. This firm admitted responsibility for the ship but were amazed that it was in West India Docks for it should have been at Surrey Docks on the other side of the river. Since this was the dock specialising in timber the crew had merely asked for "timber wharves".

At this point the dockmaster took over and told the firm to send someone down to the lockside with £50 in cash, for this was the charge for raising and lowering the water in the lock unnecessarily. Only on receipt of their money would he release the ship.

There were three pairs of lock gates on the main lock into India and Millwall Docks, one pair at each end and a further pair roughly in the middle. This meant that should one of the end pairs be under repair, then the middle pair could be brought into operation enabling all but the biggest ships to still use the lock. This arrangement was known as 'working half lock' and could also be used if there were only small ships due to use the lock. But what happened if two sets of gates were out of action?

A small coaster came into the lock to pass out into the river. Nothing else was in the lock. The skipper rang down from the bridge for slow astern to take the way off the ship ready for mooring up in the lock. Down below, the engineer misinterpreted the signal and put the ship full ahead. The vessel charged the outer gates, more or less demolishing them. So the half lock system was introduced while they were repaired.

A couple of days later, either the Suecia or the Britannia locked in on her regular run from Gothenburg. As she left the lock her propeller caught a rope trailing from the dolphin, which served to protect the inner gate. This pulled the gate from its position against the lock wall, damaging the mechanism that controlled it. So that was two sets of lock gates out of action.

A partial solution was found by using the Blackwall entrance, usually reserved for lighters and other small craft, to admit and exit the smaller ships. But anything of any size had to be diverted to the Royal Docks. There were also a number of large ships trapped within the India and Millwall system. These were, of course, still working cargo and their owners and agents were not immediately worried. But, after about three weeks, the lock was still not ready and head office instructed that the trapped ships should be charged rent for their extended and perfectly unintentional stay in the docks. This, of course, caused a furore with the usual farce of charges being rendered and then withdrawn as head office came to realise their own mistake. Only the PLA's image was damaged, as usual.

Underwater work on the lock gates was performed by the PLA's own team of divers, many of whom were ex-naval divers, very often using an odd-shaped object called a limpet. This, I believe, was a primitive diving bell. The divers were also, in conjunction with the salvage service, responsible for removing objects from the floor of the dock. There was the occasional sunken lighter, but the most common objects were unwanted cars tipped into the dock as an easy way of disposal. One of my visiting lighterage foremen was embarrassed when describing his new car. When asked what happened to the old one he became evasive and was then informed that an exactly similar model had been pulled out of the dock the previous day, though since the number plates were missing nothing could be proved.

One of the largest objects rescued from the dock was a mobile crane. The report on the incident stated that the driver when trying to reach an object aboard a lighter had toppled the crane into the water "in an excess of zeal". Fortunately the driver jumped clear and received only a ducking.

Blackwall entrance as I have mentioned dealt primarily with small craft and was looked upon as a sort of holiday camp for lockmen. It certainly worked to its own set of rules. One of these was that the last lock-in of the day would be at 7.30 in the evening. Lightermen were allowed about half an hour after locking in to moor their craft safely for the night. This meant that they were on overtime until 8pm. However, if they conducted a 'whip round' for the lock staff, the lock in would still occur at 7.30 but be booked as 7.45, thereby entitling the lightermen to be paid a 'short night'. i.e. overtime until 10pm plus an allowance for tea. So everybody did very nicely, never mind the waste of lighterage company money.

The dockmaster controlled two tugs, Beverly and Dollar Bay. Both were described as ship towage tugs and Beverly gave yeoman service at this task but Dollar Bay was a poor old thing, frequently under repair and was usually to be found pulling strings of lighters out of the Blackwall entrance. Even so she was sometimes given a small ship to play with if Beverly was otherwise engaged.

Beverly did much of her work with tugs of the private ship towage companies, by then reduced to two main ones – W. H. J. Alexander and Ship Towage Ltd., which was a combination of several companies, each retaining its own livery and system of naming its tugs. Generally two tugs would be required for a ship of any size, one at each end. It was the tug at the stern that had the worst job, as in this position a tug could become 'girt', being dragged along sideways, in imminent danger of capsizing. This was why tugs, at any rate in London, always towed on rope with an axe stowed close handy to the towing hook so that the tow could be cut if a 'girt' situation developed.

Generally dues on sail training ships were waived as were normal towage charges but a nominal charge of £10 was made for the use of the tug's towline. Whether this went back to the days when the London tugs went 'seeking' into the English Channel, hoping to pick up inward bound clippers, I do not know, but it seems a good theory.

There were two dry docks within the India and Millwall complex, one privately run and the other, at Millwall Dock, under PLA control. Although firms of ship repairers carried out repairs to ships in the Millwall Dry Dock, the PLA was responsible for the operation of the dock. A dockmaster would see the ship into the dock and a foreman with a gang of dry dock hands would see to the draining of the water from the dock and the shoring up of the vessel. The whole process would be reversed when the ship left the dry dock. Then a document called a stemming order would be prepared and sent to the dues office where it formed the basis of the bill for the use of the dry dock.

It was stemming orders that revealed just how much overtime the dry dock foreman was doing. It was virtually every Sunday. If there was no ship in the dry dock, he and his gang had maintenance work to do, if there was a ship in with the ship repairers working they had to be there in case they were needed. But best of all was the situation with a ship in but not being worked upon. Then the foreman was required to check that ship repairers were not working after all. This he did by driving his car round the perimeter of the dry dock just before noon. Having established that nothing was going on, he would then park at the pub opposite and have a few lunchtime beers before returning home. Seven hours at double pay! Nice work if you could get it!

LABOUR RELATIONS

I cannot pretend to be an expert on this subject, but I suppose I was closer than many to the 'shop floor' in the docks, especially later on when I administered payrolls, firstly for a big firm of stevedores who were 'partners in computer development with the PLA' and later for the PLA themselves.

Earlier I agreed with the majority view that the dockers would strike at any time over any grievance. But if the history of dock labour is studied, one comes to accept they had every reason to adopt the attitude they did. The way their grandfathers were treated was disgusting and, I believe that psychologically, they feared that those days might return.

Back in the days of the dock companies, employment was entirely dependent on the work available. With sailing ships predominating, a foul wind for coming up channel would mean that the available work in the docks was drastically reduced. Those wishing to work would present themselves at the morning 'call', hoping to be taken on, but most were disappointed and no work meant no pay at that time. This could lead to fights for the available jobs and to attempts at subversion, such as plying the 'call' foreman with drinks the night before in the hope of favourable treatment the next day.

By my time, things had considerably improved, but were still by no means perfect. A hard core of dockers was permanently employed and were generally referred to as 'perms'. The rest were casual labour but when not working received a basic wage from the National Dock Labour Board. This was soon changed so that all had guaranteed permanent jobs. The drawback was that as an employer went out of business, his labour force was reallocated among the other employers. At first this worked well. If, say, a small lighterage firm closed down, then the larger lighterage companies could absorb its few employees without trouble. But the effect was cumulative and larger and larger firms shut until the PLA was left as an 'employer of last resort,' having to pay a surplus of labour that it didn't really need.

In the 1960s Jack Dash emerged as the dockers' leader. Many hard things have been said about Jack, but one had to admire his dedication. I never met him personally, although he was on one of my payrolls for a time he was continually absent without pay. Those that did meet him privately said that he was a very nice man, once off his soapbox.

Later in my career, I had personal contact with many dockers and found them easy enough to get on with, provided that you treated them as equals and did not attempt to talk down to them. The strange thing was that if a strike was in progress, they nearly all said that they did not agree with it and wanted to get back to work. Such was their loyalty to one another that it was definitely 'one out, all out'. In fact I have heard of a gang loading a sailing barge being told that there was a strike and immediately walking off, without enquiring what the strike was about. One saying, current at that time, was that if each docker were given a bar of gold, they would be back within weeks demanding another one.

In fact, so petty and numerous did disputes become, that there was at least one instance of someone attempting to play the dockers at their own game. A PLA supervisor returned from a meeting to find the labour force for his ship streaming off. He stopped a group of dockers and asked what the dispute was about and received the reply: "Dunno. Strike, ain't it?"

He then contacted a shop steward who bluntly refused to tell him what the strike was about. This was too much. The supervisor went aboard the ship and climbed down into the hold, informing his foreman that he would only come out when the labour force returned. "I'm only playing their game," he said.

His superior arrived and requested that he come out of the hold. "Only when the men come back," he insisted. Thereafter higher and higher officials requested that he quit the hold, but he refused and was only persuaded to come out (under protest) by the dock manager himself. The dispute was allowed to run its course and the supervisor transferred to London Docks, then thought to be the penal colony for those in operational jobs. But it did him no harm for he eventually retired as assistant docks manager, London Docks.

The tally clerks were a particularly militant group within the docks. The basic tally clerk job was counting. goods coming off a ship were counted twice, once by a tally clerk representing the ship owner (overside tally clerk or OST) and again by a shore-based tally clerk representing the PLA. The two tallies had to agree and any disputes had to be settled.

A story demonstrates this process. A ship arrived from the Far East carrying three live elephants. These were put ashore in slings by a heavy lift derrick. Afterwards the ship tally read: Elephants, three, while the shore tally gave: Elephants, two. Wags suggested that the dock water be searched for the corpse of an elephant.

But that was the basic tally clerk job, they carried out several other functions including the preparation of ship's plans for export cargoes. This was a very complicated job, as the goods shipped had to come out in the right order at the other end of the voyage. Restowing of cargo represented time wasted and time in the shipping business is money. The ship might be calling at a dozen small ports and it was no good putting cargo for the third port under cargo for the twelfth port. Due allowance had to be made for special items such as hazardous cargo, heavy lifts or items that could only be carried on deck. So there were some clever men among the ranks of the tally clerks and I knew of at least one who had a degree.

But what the dockers obtained, the tally clerks wanted. This principle was fair enough when it came to pay and conditions, but reached ridiculous levels on some things. For example when the dockers received free gloves to protect their hands, the tally clerks started a long campaign for a glove issue for themselves. The basic tally clerk job was about writing and who can write effectively wearing gloves?

The dockers' attitude went on upwards and affected the staff. A sensible rule was passed which said that on a Sunday, if work was in progress, a first-aider must be present. Now most of the shed writers were qualified as first-aiders and the management said that if the writer on duty to do his normal job was so qualified, then there was no need for a separate man to cover

173

first-aid. But the union would not agree so two writers were in attendance with one of them with nothing to do unless there was an injury and the shipping company had to pay accordingly.

Then there was the strike of the 'Pentonville Five'. This was originally about the use of non-registered labour at cold stores within the accepted hinterland of the docks. The dockers maintained that this should be their work but the employers felt that it was not dock-work and that they could save money by employing non-dockers. The dispute reached such a pitch that the five dockers leaders ended up in Pentonville prison. Then everybody walked out – tug crews, lockmen, foremen, and even canteen staff. The only people left at work were the salaried staff and the police, plus three foremen who had had the courage of their convictions and come to work but who had to be locked up in the personnel department for their own protection. For a couple of days a siege mentality set in as the remaining staff wondered how long it would be before they were prevented from reporting for work.

Then the Official Solicitor stepped in and freed the Five. The dispute was settled and dockers were allowed to work at the cold stores, although naturally not all those projected were ever established within the five mile corridor that dockers claimed was theirs.

Not all disputes were about money or the available work, some were about hours. In the 1960s Saturday mornings became an issue and a compromise was reached. The dockers were only required to work two hours on Saturdays (8-10am). But in practice they were allowed half an hour at the start and finish of each work period for the ship's crew and the stevedores to remove the ship's beams and hatches. So Saturday then consisted of half an hour's waiting while the ship was made ready, an extended 'muggo' or tea-break and then another half hour's waiting (allegedly) while beams and hatches were replaced without any work being done at all. Needless to say this system did not last very long and the dockers achieved their object of no more Saturday work, unless it was seven hours at double time.

In the case of staff, we were originally allowed just six

A new use for docks. Yachts looking out of St. Katherine's Dock

Author's collection

Saturdays off per year, known as 'red' Saturdays since they were marked in this colour on our leave forms.

There was a twilight area about Saturdays taken as part of annual leave and consequently endless argument about who owed what in Saturday attendance. So we were very pleased to receive every other Saturday off when the dockers went onto their two-hour morning. But the downside was that we had to start at 8am on Mondays, not very funny after a hectic weekend of sailing and associated activities. In vain I pleaded with our principal clerk to be allowed to do the extra hour on a Wednesday or Thursday. No doubt his Tibetan monk told him not to consider such requests and the most that he would concede was 8.30am on Monday and Tuesday.

We ended Saturday work at the same time as the dockers but the management took it right to the wire and on Thursday those due in on Saturday still did not know whether to come in or not. Just in time we got our Saturdays off, but seven hours at double

175

time was not an option for a long time.

But it was not just the dockers' strikes that eventually brought the London Docks down – there was also weak management. Colonel Oram, the PLA's operations manager, wrote a very good book on the subject when he retired called 'The Dockers' Tragedy'. Obviously he has much to say about the dockers' attitudes but he also points out that the structure of the PLA was not conducive to positive decision making.

The Port of London in the 1950s, 60s and 70s was a public trust run by a board. It could issue stock but not shares. The board was comprised of 'interested parties' in the port – predominantly ship owners and shippers of goods. There were a few other organisations represented such as the lighterage trade and the dock labour. So the Port of London was virtually run by its own customers who were not likely to agree to anything against their own interests. In fact it was not unknown for a member of the staff to be told by a disgruntled representative of a customer: "One of our directors is also on the board of the PLA. What's your name? I'll mention it to him." The threat was obvious.

The attitude of ship-owners was, more or less, the quicker their ships were turned round the better. As I said earlier 'time is money' in the shipping business. A good example of this occurred at South West India Dock. A ship that was discharging was expected in Antwerp in time to start work on Monday morning. By lunchtime on the Friday it became obvious that not all the cargo would be out of her even if the dockers worked until 7pm. The ship-owner contacted the superintendent in charge of the ship and asked how much would the dockers want to work on to a finish.

The superintendent had his doubts whether they would be prepared to do this but nevertheless summoned the shop steward and asked him to put the proposition to the men. Sometime later the shop steward returned and the superintendent asked him for an answer.

"I don't want to tell you," replied the shop steward. "I've never heard the like in twenty years in this dock."

The superintendent persisted and was unwillingly told a sum

that shocked him into silence.

"What they'd really like," the shop steward went on, "is all day Sunday to finish the ship."

"But the shipping company wants the ship in Antwerp for Monday," said the superintendent, "so I'd better let them know, but it's a formality. They're not going to pay that sort of money."

He rang back to the ship owner's man who merely said: "Pay it". This certainly solved his immediate problem but set a precedent for similar situations, which the dockers were unlikely to forget.

Because of this type of thing, decision-making was curtailed and red tape abounded. The business of the towage orders being detached and their accompanying document being endorsed is one example. Here is another. A colleague of mine had been on West India Dock import ledgers for practically the whole of his career. What he did not know about import ledgers was not worth knowing and he was, deservedly, promoted to be the import ledger specialist at head office.

There he quietly got on with the job, occasionally phoning a shed foreman at West India Dock when he wanted advice from the shop floor. He had known this foreman for years and they had become friends. One day he was summoned to see his boss and quickly realised that he was on the carpet.

"Mr. Smith," said the boss severely, "I understand that you have been phoning a foreman at West India Dock about the work." He confirmed that he had and was then told that this was entirely contrary to accepted procedure.

"If you want information from the docks," the boss went on, "you must send a memo to the docks superintendent. He will then contact the senior officer at the department concerned. If it is then necessary to involve a foreman then he will be contacted."

Yes, thought Smith and, if I am lucky, I will get an answer in two weeks instead of two minutes. But that was the way it had to be, at the time. Happily there was some relaxation of this type of rule within a few years.

Some shipping companies were very particular and would

check every detail of a discharging or loading account. Arguments over a penny were not uncommon with this variety. Others, however, went to the opposite extreme. One day the West India Dues Office had a phone call from a very big shipping company in Liverpool who had a large and regular trade into the dock. Normally we did not hear from them at all. A very laid back gentleman enquired whether we could explain why the costs of one of their ships had shot up from 2d a ton to 3d a ton. He said that he was curious about this but that he was going to pass the discharging account for payment anyway. We said that we could not give him an immediate answer but that we would look into it.

Then all hands took the discharging account apart. At first we were baffled for there was nothing untoward and the details of the account compared favourably with those of other ships of the line in the same trade. Then somebody looked at the summary of the account on the first page. There was an addition error of £6,000!

The man in Liverpool was telephoned back and abject apologies made. We would send him a credit note for £6000.

"Oh, don't worry about it," he said. "These things happen. As a matter of fact we don't bother to check your accounts. They're always accurate, so we just divide tons into money as a rough guide." And this from a company renowned for paying and feeding its crews badly!

Once I had moved onto working out loading accounts for ships one of the items I found that I had to recover from shipping companies was the cost of our labour standing by when unable to work through no fault of their own. Any rain (or snow) lasting more than half an hour was one of these items. But I eventually became puzzled for it seemed to rain in different parts of the dock at different times.

In the end there was a long period of fine weather but 'rain' still appeared on some loading accounts. I showed one such account to the shed writer who had prepared it. He was somewhat embarrassed.

"We've got to show it like that," he said. "The shipping

company would not stand for it if they knew the real reason. Look, the ship's clerk has signed for it and they'll take his word for it. Just bung it in anyway. It'll be all right." And so it proved.

Overtime was also recoverable. One shipping company that was known to be particularly 'sticky' was billed for an hour's overtime for the quay gang on the grounds that the last set of cargo had not landed on the quay until two minutes past five. The bill was promptly returned with the claim that the set had left the ship at two minutes to five. So where had it been for four minutes? The implication was that the dockers had deliberately delayed it in mid-air. But the argument was hardly fair as, even had it landed before five o'clock, there was still the matter of removing the slings and returning the crane to its resting position.

Much has been said about containers being introduced because of the troubles with dock labour. This is, at best, only partly true. Containers had been around for some time before the

The spread of containers. A 'reefer' partly loaded with containers
Author's collection

'container revolution'. They had been known in coastal trades since before World War II and were listed separately in Lloyd's Register of Shipping. The thought was, probably, like the rail containers then carried on flatbed railway wagons they could be transferred to lorries for door-to-door deliveries.

The container revolution involved sophisticated and expensive equipment for the loading and discharge of containers. It was not just a question of loading a ship with containers using the ship's own gear. Eventually fewer men were required, but they had to be prepared to work a round the clock shift system, seven days a week and be capable of operating complicated machinery. It also has to be borne in mind that a modern container ship carries as much cargo in containers as many conventional ships, so there is considerable saving in ships and crews as well as dock labour.

AND FINALLY...

It was originally my intention only to cover the first thirty odd of my years in this book. On reflection, though, it is perhaps only fair to bring the reader more or less up to date. All things change in time but, happily, some retain much of the original.

A case in point is the older part of Leigh-on-Sea. It has survived numerous threats to its continued existence plus sheer unnecessary vandalism from the local authority that, at one time, destroyed several delightful buildings for no apparent reason. Fortunately in these days of conservation they now know better.

A bridge over the railway now gives access to Old Leigh but, while maintaining the atmosphere of a fishing village, it has become rather twee, with many gift shops and eating-places. There are still boats fishing although the fleet is greatly reduced and one wonders how much longer it will last as the creek is silting up and modern fishing methods require quick turn rounds. Now and again one of the surviving boats goes after white-weed which is still caught the same way.

Modern sea defences should ensure that there is no repetition of the 1953 floods and the opportunity was taken to install pedestrian walkways when the seawalls were raised. All the pubs are still there and the Crooked Billet often wins awards both for its beer and its floral decorations. Barges still come to Leigh now and again but usually to host either a wedding reception or a shanty concert.

Over on the marshes, however, Les Warland's yard is long gone. Eventually the council caught up with Les and, since he was not prepared and could not afford to pay rates, the yard had to go. None of his lighters was capable of floating for very long and so they were broken up on site, which must have a very unpleasant job. Les endeavoured to carry on for a while, using a former Dutch barge as his headquarters, but was eventually forced to become skipper of Len Johnson's yacht Lady Leigh and give up being a self-employed boat builder. It is still possible, when standing on the seawall, to make out the pattern of the paths that used to connect the elements of his yard.

However, between the site of the yard and the new bridge to Two

Tree Island, a new enterprise has sprung up. This is the headquarters and yard of Leigh Motor Club, a thriving organisation for motorboat owners who do not wish to sail. Their members lay their boats up in the yard and work on them themselves, presumably a different proposition to a 'commercially' run yard.

Leigh Sailing Club is still in the Old Station buildings, now very much altered with a saloon upstairs complete with veranda and the former 'railway' rooms converted to changing rooms and showers. Some years ago the railway attempted to sell the building at auction without much notice. At the last minute the club was able to get the 'lot' withdrawn and then negotiated to buy the lease. In this it was successful, but it had to take out a huge loan to complete the sale. Some headway had been made in repaying this when considerable dry rot was discovered in the lower part of the clubhouse. This was put right, with the cost being added to the mortgage. The repayments became almost too much for the club to meet and it went through a number of lean years until interest rates fell and a number of strokes of financial good

'Boy Martin' – a recent picture

Nick Hann collection

182

fortune enabled the club to clear the mortgage entirely.

The dinghies are still kept on racks, now considerably enlarged and with an extra set down at Chalkwell where the races are still started. But there have been so many repairs and alterations over the years, it is doubtful whether anything remains of the originals. Also added was an enclosure known to all as 'The Birdcage' at the east end of the club-house. This was originally intended as storage for boats that were in transit or laid up for the winter. The rules were that those in the Birdcage for the winter had to quit by the end of April and, in my early days as club sailing secretary, I had to administer both the racks and the Birdcage.

It was through looking after the Birdcage that I came to meet my wife, Margaret. I had had my eye on a clinker-built sailing dinghy that had been in the Birdcage for the winter but was still there in May, although obviously being worked on. One day I found a young lady painting this boat.

"Why is this boat still here?" I wanted to know.

"Because I'm still working on it," she said sweetly.

I explained the rules about winter storage but she said she had been unaware of them and, in any case, her boat was not going in the water until it was ready. I think that I threatened to charge her for summer storage as well and wandered off. Somewhat annoyed she went in the club-house and, after buying herself a drink, settled with a group of people who she did not know but looked as though they might be sympathetic. She told them the story, complaining about the draconian attitude of the sailing secretary.

One of the group said: "Yes, he does get a bit above himself."

'Wylurheer'

Dent family collection

At that moment, I arrived, walked over to Margaret's new friends and asked: "Would you like a drink … mother, father, aunt, cousin James, uncle?" Aghast, Margaret realised that she had sat down with my family! That was our first encounter. There were, of course, plenty more and, a few years later, we were married. We had two children, a girl and a boy. Helen has inherited my love of things nautical but is now married and lives well away from the sea. Alex is interested but has plenty of other things to do, including a high-powered job.

EODs and TEODs are no longer sailed at Leigh. Some years ago the best points of both boats were amalgamated into a new class, known as the Estuary One Designs, built of fibreglass and, at first, referred to by their detractors as 'Plastic One Designs'. Many of the TEODs were bought by a character known as 'The Mad Major' and taken away for a new career in Scotland where some of them may still be sailing. One, Mistral, which I sailed on in Burnham Week, is permanently laid up near Leigh. EODs fared rather better and there are still one or two of the old wooden boats sailing with the Estuary One Designs at the Essex

Mirrors racing at Leigh

Author's collection

184

Yacht Club.

Very recently the GP 14s have declined after over forty years racing with the Club. Their likely replacement is likely to be the RS 400, which is a very much 'go faster' dinghy. There are currently about twelve of these owned within the club. My own involvement with the GP 14 came to an end when Margaret and I, with a baby on the way, both sold our boats. I assumed that I could find plenty of crewing jobs or even helm for somebody else. But this did not work out and I had my poorest sailing season ever. So I just had to get another boat!

A boat that I had tried out that year was the Mirror dinghy. I liked its sailing qualities a lot and it was described to me as an ideal family boat. During the following winter I heard that my doctor was selling one, so we wheeled Helen in her pram round to the doctor's house to inspect this boat. It was in excellent condition and only two years old, so I bought it on the spot.

When I inquired about its name the doctor told me that it was Wylurheer. I then asked where such an unusual name came from. The doctor said that when he made house calls and had finished with the main patient, he was often asked: "While you're here, doctor, could you look at little Johnny's ear, big toe, boil, etc." So used had he become to this form of approach he felt that its corrupted form would make an appropriate name for his boat. I felt that it was bad luck to change a boat's name and so kept Wylurheer as, I believe, the present owner has done. I sailed this Mirror for thirty-one years, both with the family and on my own and had a lot of fun from her. But I haven't given up and have recently bought a 'new' second-hand Mirror.

The London Docks doesn't really exist anymore. The Port of London Authority, having absorbed the pilotage function of Trinity House some years ago, is now solely a harbour authority with headquarters in Gravesend. Tilbury Docks are still working largely with containers and forest products, but were the subject of a management buy out about ten years ago and later were taken over by the Port of Forth Authority.

To return to my own experience, what was thought to be a great opportunity at the time was offered in the early 1960s. Promotion to executive officer was to be by examination, not by interview! The examination was to consist of three subjects, English, geography and PLA practice. All three had to be passed and an overall pass mark obtained, then the interviews happened anyway! PLA interviews were dreaded in those days. They were generally conducted by a panel of three, a neutral chairman, a representative of the personnel department, who would usually ask the candidate what books they read or some other mild personal question and not much more, and a third member who was the one to fear. Very often a gentleman who had a title like 'principal executive officer' occupied this position and so far as we staff could see, his sole employment was sitting on interview panels. One of his typical tactics would be to say: "Now, Mr. Dent, you have applied for a position in the accounting department, so tell me how do you see the future of the authority's dredging unit?"

Various helpful suggestions were made by colleagues about how to succeed at a PLA interview, such as imagining the panel naked or making great use of your one friend in the interview room – the chair that you were about to sit on.

I cannot remember whether I employed either of these tactics, but at the third attempt, I survived both the executive officer exam and the interview and was placed on a list to be promoted when a vacancy arose. I must have been at the bottom of the list for the summons to head office was a long time coming.

Eventually I was told to report to the accounting department at head office. I held a farewell party for my West India Dock friends in an odd pub outside the dock, which never had any other customers, but, the landlord assured us it was much livelier in the evenings when the homosexuals were there. At the time the Three Degrees were at the top of the charts with 'Baby Love' and this continually played on the pub's jukebox by my colleagues and I will forever associate it with leaving West India Dock.

The following Monday I reported to the staff clerk of the accounting department and found that I was one of two new executive officers arriving to fill two vacancies. The staff clerk explained that one of these was in general accounting and the other in data processing. Did either of us have any preference? Neither of us had a clue about the duties of either section so the matter was decided by the flip of a coin and I drew data processing the main task of which was the production of payrolls. Little did I suspect that I was to remain in this department for the rest of my PLA career, surviving several changes of location and methods of working and gaining several promotions.

Despite the awe in which dock staff held head office staff, nothing had really changed. I was still surrounded by characters. Frank, our manager, was somewhat of a mystery man. He had a military bearing and looked every inch an army officer. Always well turned out, he frequently sported a regimental tie. Eventually the rumours were pieced together and the story was that he had been 'Officer in charge of mule transport' for Orde Wingate's Chindits in Burma, winning the Military Medal. But we never heard this from Frank himself.

In fact Frank kept a lot to himself. We never knew that he was a car driver until he once looked in during Saturday overtime and left wearing leather gloves and a flat cap, looking just like a motorist of the old school. Someone nipped down to the car park exit and saw him drive away. But, again, he never mentioned the car himself. With perfect timing, he took voluntary severance just as the accounting department moved to Royal Docks. He had never worked in the docks and we just couldn't imagine him doing so.

Then there was Boots, who ran the payroll for salaried staff. His nickname was either a corruption of his real name, a reference to the large number of pills kept in his desk or to the fact that he invariably wore boots. There was a war between Frank and Boots about the untidiness of the latter's desk. One day when Frank was particularly persistent about the piles of paper on the desk, Boots pushed back his chair and said, in exasperation: "Frank, there is a system. I know which dog ear is which." Frank walked away.

Pat was an Irishman whose father had been a hero of the Easter Uprising. He would sit at his desk and rant about " the crimes of the bloody English", forgetting that he was entirely surrounded by Englishmen. We thought best not to argue with him.

As the Port of London declined the head office function moved ever eastward. My career in data processing started at the PLA Building overlooking Tower Hill in an area known as 'the Rotunda'. The original had been a gold adorned annexe in the central quadrangle of the building but had been destroyed during the Blitz. Its replacement was a prefabricated-type structure.

We were there just about long enough for me to learn my new job and then moved to a purpose built building in St. Katharine's Dock.

Warehouses at West India Dock, now to be the Docklands Museum

Author's collection

This was indeed luxury. The ground floor was the police headquarters and the second and third floors housed the accounting department and the computer department. But the first floor contained all the amenities the staff could wish for. Most of it was given over to the canteen and its kitchens but there was also a bar, a shop, a snooker room, a table tennis room and a lounge or television room. All of these amenities were provided not just for those working in the building, but also for all PLA staff in London.

Moreover we were working in an interesting area. Close by were the Tower of London and Tower Bridge, thronged with tourists. When out for a walk at lunchtime, I was often approached for directions or to take a photo of a family group posed in front of one of the historic buildings. Probably the most memorable incident came when a Japanese thrust a London tube map in front of me with the request "Blitish Museum?" Since he had no further English, I was unable to help him.

I frequently walked on to Tower Bridge during the lunch hour to watch the river traffic. This included tugs and lighters that I remembered from my days as a dues clerk. It was easy enough to spot those carrying grain for they always followed by a cloud of pigeons. This reminded me of the war against these birds at Central Granary, Millwall Docks.

It had been triggered by a letter from a prominent producer of breakfast cereals who received complete trainloads of grain from the granary. It stated that, whereas the firm expected to find the odd dead pigeon among its grain, they did object to a complete railway wagon of nests, eggs, droppings and dead birds. Could we please reduce the pigeon population of the Millwall Granary? Various methods were employed in an attempt to comply with this reasonable request. Shooting was too slow although it was satisfying to the staff employed and jelly that made the birds feel unstable was hit and miss, since there were thousands of possible perches within the building. By far the best deterrent was a hawk, but this was an extremely expensive method. In the end, all concerned including the cereal company gave up. Pigeons were accepted as a necessary evil.

But the idyll at St. Katharine's only lasted a few years. As the PLA contracted and more and more operating departments closed, the head office function declined. Our building was largely sold off to become the World Trade Centre and we moved to premises at the basin, Royal Docks that I thought resembled a prison camp in many respects. They contained none of the staff amenities that we had grown used to and

The author aboard the sailing barge 'Reminder'

Author's collection

even the canteen was a fair walk away. We consoled ourselves with the use of various beer cupboards and, on fine summer days I would take sandwiches on to the pier head and watch the now much decreased river traffic.

Inevitably we moved on after a few years to Tilbury Docks. This was better for we were accommodated in a new custom-built computer centre and, of course, my travelling was shorter and cheaper. To my delight, I was sent to Tilbury before the rest to supervise the transfer of a large stevedoring company to the PLA payrolls. The only snag at Tilbury was an even longer walk to the canteen. It was only just possible to have a meal, visit the bank, which was just outside the dock gates and get back to the office in an hour.

And at Tilbury I remained until the PLA was split up into small units prior to privatisation. At that point I was made an offer that I could not refuse to take early retirement and then joined Customs and Excise in Southend to do a small part-time job.

Despite the usual exchange of addresses, I never saw anyone that I was in the Navy with again – with two small exceptions. One of these occurred during Burnham Week at a function held by the Crouch Yacht Club about two years after I was demobbed. I suddenly realised that I was standing next to somebody that I recognised and he must have thought the same for we both said "Royal Navy" at the same time.

He was one of the would-be officer candidates from my basic training. He told me that he had eventually become an officer and had left with the exalted rank of sub-lieutenant. But then he went on to spoil things by telling me that he had borrowed daddy's 40-footer for Burnham Week. He asked me what I was sailing and I told him that I was crewing on a TEOD.

"Oh, they're an open boat, aren't they?" he said, his eyes appearing to glaze over. I confirmed this and he wandered off to rejoin his friends.

The second encounter occurred in the bar of Leigh Sailing Club. It was Friday night and the bar was quite crowded, when a voice called "Hi! Dicky!" Now, as I have mentioned, Dicky was my nickname in Chatham Barracks and was unknown in the sailing club, but I automatically turned round and could not trace the source of the voice. So I walked down the bar to try and find out more and encountered an outstretched hand. I shook it, still mystified and its owner said: "It is

190

Dicky from Chatham Barracks, isn't it?" The man was evidently a visitor to the club but I still could not place him. He explained that he was Petty Officer Brown (or a similar common name) and that I had often given him an early shake with a cup of tea when he had been duty petty officer.

Now I had performed this favour for possibly a hundred duty POs and certainly did not remember him but the nickname was authentic and from other things that he said he was genuine, all right. It transpired that he wished to join the club with a view to acting as coxswain of the safety boat and, since there was a distinct shortage of coxswains at the time, his offer was gladly accepted. But it transpired that his idea of running the boat was to take along his wife, family and fishing gear and this would have been no good at all in an emergency when lives might have to be saved. So his tenure of the coxswain's position and his club membership were brief.

Readers will, I'm sure, have noticed the several references to the Thames barge in these pages. Early on I refer to my interest in these craft as being akin to train spotting, but it has been an enduring fascination which has not ended, although there are no longer any working barges to follow. There is much to research, such as the history of barges long since dismantled, trading patterns and the location of wharves where barges used to trade. In the 1970s I joined the Society for Sailing Barge Research, which was founded in 1963 to explore all these avenues of research and many others. These days it is flourishing as more and more people wish to learn 'what granddad did on the barges' and students choose the Thames barge and its history as a subject for a thesis. I have been on the society's committee for some years and am currently their Treasurer and deal with my fair share of enquiries as detailed above. I have also written about the Thames barge in articles and short stories as well as lecturing on the subject. I am also the author of two books about the vessel – 'The Third Hand', a novel, and 'Tidal Tales', a collection of short stories. It all leads to a busy retirement!

Despite all the 'office' work on the Thames barge, I have only occasionally sailed on one. Probably this is in keeping with the title of this book – "Not Quite at Sea"!

THE END